The Giant American History Timeline

Book 1
Pre-Colonization–Reconstruction

Sunflower education

★ TABLE OF CONTENTS ★

★ Unit 1 ★ Discovery and Exploration: Prehistory–1606

✭ Unit 2 ✭ Colonial America: 1585–1776

✭ Unit 3 ✭ The Revolutionary Period: 1765–1783

⋆ Unit 4 ⋆ Creating the Constitution: 1781–1803

⋆ Unit 5 ⋆ Expanding the Country: 1790–1860

★ Unit 6 ★ An Age of Advancements: 1790–1860

★ Unit 7 ★ Social Issues: 1790–1860

★ Unit 8 ★ The Civil War and Reconstruction: 1850–1877

★ Assessments ★

★ Answer Key ★

★ Introduction ★

Most parents/teachers are all too familiar with students who can recite facts without understanding them within a historical context. *The Giant American History Timeline 1* is designed to give students an overall understanding of American history. Specific facts make sense to students when presented within a larger context.

The unique approach used in *The Giant American History Timeline 1* makes American history accessible for students of varying ages and abilities. Your students will enjoy researching and presenting facts about significant events, people, and places in American history while completing the high-interest activity sheets in each unit. Students will then help you create a detailed timeline to display in the classroom or hallway. As students progress through the program, they will modify and expand the timeline so that it progresses with them.

The timeline approach allows students to see how much they have learned as their work is displayed and provides them with an organized, ongoing review of the material presented. Students will work individually and in groups to create visual presentations they can prominently and proudly display.

The Giant American History Timeline 1 will allow you to:

- create detailed timelines for specific periods in American history;
- customize the timelines to meet your students' needs;
- use the timelines to help students understand historical patterns; and
- emphasize students' development of essential critical thinking skills.

While completing activity sheets and assembling timelines, students will practice critical thinking skills such as identifying main ideas and details, sequencing events, and relating causes and effects. For students to have a solid understanding of history, they must be able to understand what happened (main ideas and details), when it happened (sequencing), and how the event relates to other things that happened (cause and effect).

This program involves students in asking questions about historical events, people, and places while guiding them to develop a complete understanding of American history.

HOW *The Giant American History Timeline 1* IS ORGANIZED

Two Books

This book is the first in a series of two. Book 1 covers the arrival of early peoples in North America through Reconstruction. Book 2 begins with the industrial growth and technological advancements after Reconstruction and covers American history through the present.

Units

This reproducible, 237-page book consists of eight units that introduce students to the beginnings of American history through Reconstruction. Units include:

Unit 1. Discovery and Exploration: Prehistory–1606

Unit 2. Colonial America: 1585–1776

Unit 3. The Revolutionary Period: 1765–1783

Unit 4. Creating the Constitution: 1781–1803

Unit 5. Expanding the Country: 1790–1860

Unit 6. An Age of Advancements: 1790–1860

Unit 7. Social Issues: 1790–1860

Unit 8. The Civil War and Reconstruction: 1850–1877

Units 1, 2, 3, 4, and 8 each address a different historical period. Units 5, 6, and 7 cover the same historical period, but each focuses on a different topic related to the period. Each unit includes a Teaching Notes section, followed by 14–18 student activity sheets.

Teaching Notes

The Teaching Notes section in each unit includes the following:

Unit Overview—an overview of the major historical developments of the period and how they are addressed on the activity sheets

Focus Activities—three activities that focus students' attention on the period being studied

Constructing the Timeline—instructions for assembling completed activity sheets to form a classroom timeline; provides diagrams for creating a basic timeline or a complete timeline

Critical Thinking Skills—a description of the critical thinking skills reinforced in the unit, both by the activity sheets and the completed timeline

Individual Activity Sheet Notes—specific instructions on guiding students through the completion and extension of each activity sheet

Activity Sheets

The activity sheets are presented in a variety of formats to make them appropriate for students of varying ability levels and learning styles and to ensure that the posted timelines are visually appealing. Students will create and complete maps, complete and extend graphic organizers, analyze primary source materials, answer questions, write captions, create graphs, compare and contrast time periods, and more.

In every unit, each activity sheet is labeled with a number and a letter that identifies the unit number as well as the activity's placement within the unit. For example, the first activity sheet in Unit 1 is labeled 1-A. The activity sheets are presented in chronological order.

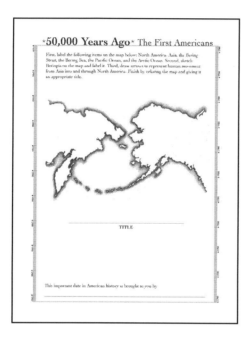

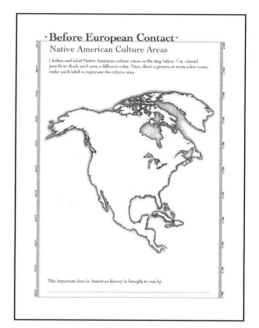

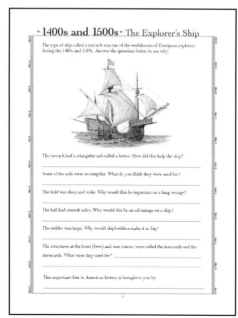

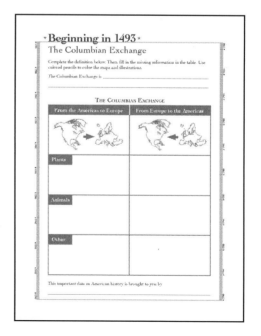

Six types of activity sheets are repeated throughout the program. These activity sheets provide historical continuity and visual cohesion within the posted timelines.

Title Activity Sheets

The first activity sheet in every unit has the same title as the unit in which it appears. As students complete these activity sheets, they generate and answer general questions about the historical periods being covered. The eight Title Activity Sheets feature the titles and main ideas of the historical periods on the posted timelines.

Map Study Activity Sheets

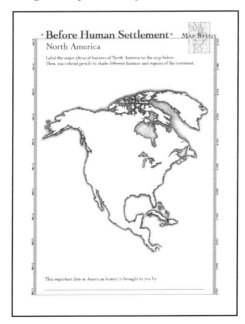

These activity sheets appear in various places within the units. Students complete a map of the United States, or in earlier units, the land that would become the United States. Some Map Study Activity Sheets also feature demographic components, asking students to analyze the U.S. population during certain time periods.

Biography Activity Sheets

BIOGRAPHY

These activity sheets appear in various places within the units. Biography Activity Sheets focus on one or more significant people from the historical period being covered.

A Voice From the Past Activity Sheets

A VOICE FROM THE PAST

These activity sheets appear in various places within the units. A Voice From the Past Activity Sheets provide students with high-interest primary source materials from the historical periods being covered.

TIME MACHINE

Time Machine Activity Sheets

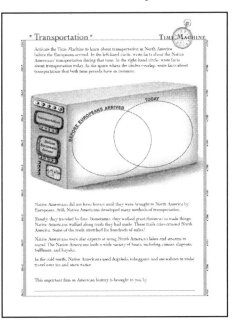

The next-to-last activity sheet in every unit addresses a high-interest social history topic. Students "set" the Time Machine to a certain topic and time period (for example, education during the colonial period) and read the information provided on the activity sheet. Then, students compare and contrast information about that topic during the time period addressed with the same topic today.

A POSTCARD FROM THE PAST

A Postcard From the Past Activity Sheets

The last activity sheet in every unit directs students to research a notable, unit-related historical site in the United States and create a postcard to "send" from that place.

USING THE ACTIVITY SHEETS

The Giant American History Timeline 1 includes 126 activity sheets that vary in topic, format, and difficulty. In every unit, suggestions for clarifying and extending the topics covered on each activity sheet are provided under the Individual Activity Sheet Notes category in the Teaching Notes Section.

As your students work through the activity sheets, keep the following guidelines in mind:

Assigning Activity Sheets

You may assign the activity sheets in any way you see fit. Students can complete each activity sheet individually, with partners, in small groups, or as a whole class. Please note that the name line at the bottom of each activity sheet is designed to give the students "classroom credit" when their work is posted as part of a timeline and to encourage the students to take pride in their accomplishments.

Completing Activity Sheets

Most activity sheets in *The Giant American History Timeline 1* require students to conduct research in order to complete them. The amount and intensity of research required varies. In some cases, students must simply recall information from class discussions or consult their textbooks to find basic facts; in other cases, students must conduct library or Internet research. After the students complete an activity sheet, encourage them to use colored pencils to shade the illustrations and maps, which will make the displayed timelines more visually appealing.

Modifying Activity Sheets

Encourage students to modify the activity sheets in appropriate ways. For example, students can add indicator lines and additional cells to graphic organizers to incorporate specific things they learned in class. They can write additional questions and the answers they find. Students can also add illustrations as appropriate.

Extending Activity Sheets

Each activity sheet can be extended in a variety of ways, such as participating in follow-up discussions, expanding graphic organizers, and conducting additional research.

UNIT ASSESSMENTS

A two-page unit assessment is provided for each unit. All eight assessments are located in the last section of the book. The first page of each assessment contains objective items and is designed to function as a basic assessment. This page focuses on the critical thinking skills of identifying main ideas and details as well as sequencing events. The second page features two short, subjective essay questions that are more difficult. One question addresses the critical thinking skill of relating causes and effects, while the other question asks students to express an opinion. For struggling students, you may wish to assign only the first page of the assessment to evaluate learning.

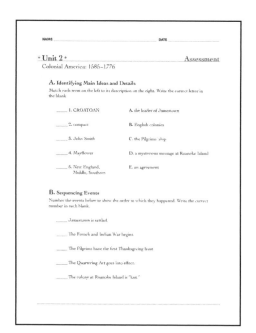

CREATING TIMELINES

The timelines created with *The Giant American History Timeline 1* consist of two basic parts: the activity sheets, completed by students, and the Timeline Components, which connect the activity sheets to form coherent timelines.

Creating timelines with *The Giant American History Timeline 1* is as easy as 1-2-3:

> **Step 1. Design the Timeline** The Teaching Notes section at the beginning of each unit provides two suggested timelines: a basic timeline (using just a few activity sheets in the unit) and a complete timeline (using all of the activity sheets in the unit). You may choose to create either one of these timelines or design your own customized timeline.

> **Step 2. Assign the Activity Sheets** Assign the activity sheets that you want to include in the timeline. Guide students as they complete the activity sheets.

> **Step 3. Construct the Timeline** Assemble the timeline on a classroom or hallway wall, attaching the activity sheets with pushpins, tape, or removable adhesive.

STUDENT PARTICIPATION

The level of student participation in creating timelines is up to you, but all three steps outlined above are amenable to student input and even student control. For example, you might guide students as they design a timeline or even assign them the task of designing the timeline themselves.

USING THE TIMELINE ARROWS

The Timeline Arrows are used to connect and show relationships among the events, people, and places that are the topics of the activity sheets. The Timeline Arrows are provided on page XVIII.

HISTORICAL RELATIONSHIPS AND CRITICAL THINKING

By positioning the arrows judiciously, it is easy to give students a sense of the connections among the activity sheet topics and reinforce the critical thinking skills of identifying main ideas and details, sequencing events, and relating causes and effects. Use formats similar to the ones shown in the diagrams on the next page to emphasize these critical thinking skills when creating timelines. Each rectangle represents a completed activity sheet, and each arrow represents a Timeline Arrow sheet.

IDENTIFYING MAIN IDEAS AND DETAILS

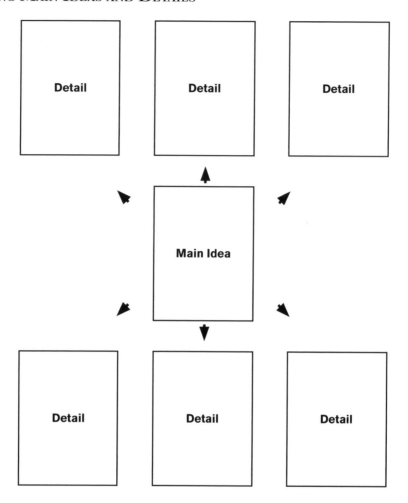

SEQUENCING EVENTS

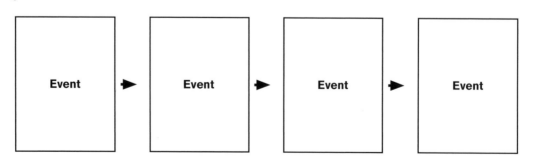

RELATING CAUSES AND EFFECTS

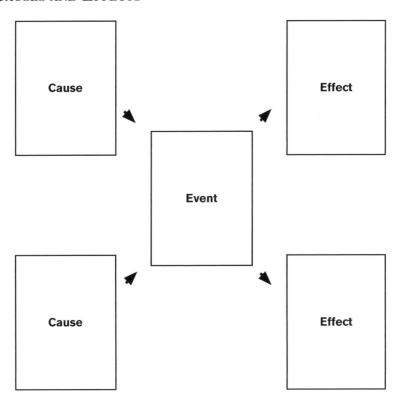

ANNOTATING THE TIMELINE ARROWS

Write words and phrases on the Timeline Arrows to clarify what they represent. For example, you might write such phrases as, "was followed by," "resulted in," and "was a main cause of," to help make the timeline more readable and the topics of the individual activity sheets less discrete. You might also direct students to color or illustrate the Timeline Arrows appropriately.

USING THE TIMELINE DATES

The Timeline Dates are used to provide a background for the events, people, and places that are the topics of the activity sheets. The Timeline Dates are provided on pages XIX–XXIV.

Most of the Timeline Dates are in quarter-century intervals. Page XIX includes relative date indicators to accommodate the broad historical spread of Unit 1. This page also includes a blank Timeline Date space to accommodate any specific need you might have.

USING THE TIMELINE SUBHEADINGS

A Title Activity Sheet provides a title for the timeline created by each unit. In addition, the timelines created by Units 6 and 7 can incorporate subheadings. The subheadings for Units 6 and 7 are provided on pages XXV–XXVI.

★ RESEARCH AND STANDARDS ★

The National Council for the Social Studies (NCSS) synthesized the "findings from the best available classroom research" and identified "an emerging consensus of expert opinion about how to teach social studies." The result is a vision for "powerful teaching and learning in the social studies," in which "powerful" refers to "ideal forms of social studies teaching and learning." According to the NCSS, social studies teaching and learning are powerful when they are: meaningful, integrative, value-based, challenging, and active.

The Giant American History Timeline 1 supports each of these key elements:

Meaningful This book creates networks—the timelines—that give meaning to American history. The NCSS writes, "Facts and ideas are not taught in isolation from other content, nor are skills. Instead, they are embedded in networks of knowledge, skills, beliefs, and attitudes that are structured around important ideas and taught emphasizing their connections.... New topics are framed with reference to where they fit within the big picture ... content is developed in ways that help students see how its elements relate to one another (e.g., using ... graphic learning aids ...)."

Integrates This book integrates knowledge of discrete historical events within the timelines. The NCSS writes, "Powerful social studies teaching is integrative across time and space, connecting with past experience ...."

Value-Based This book exposes students to different points of view about historical events in various activity sheets. The NCSS writes, "Powerful social studies teaching encourages recognition of opposing points of view ...."

Challenges This book provides appropriate individual challenging in activity sheets and fosters collaborative learning as students combine the sheets to construct the timelines. The NCSS writes, "Students ... strive to accomplish instructional goals both as individuals and as group members ... Students ... respond thoughtfully to one another's ideas."

Actively This book lets students active construct timelines that form a network of understanding about American history. The NCSS writes, "Students develop new understanding through a process of construction. They do not passively receive or copy curriculum content ... they strive to make sense of what they are learning by developing a network of connections that link the new content to preexisting knowledge ...."

The Giant American History Timeline 1 meets both state and NCSS national social studies standards. As students construct the timelines, they will fulfill major aspects of all major social studies strands identified by the NCSS.

- Strand I: Culture
- Strand II: Time, Continuity, and Change
- Strand III: People, Places, and Environments
- Strand IV: Individual Development and Identity
- Strand V: Individuals, Groups, and Institutions
- Strand VI: Power, Authority, and Governance
- Strand VII: Production, Distribution, and Consumption
- Strand VIII: Science, Technology, and Society
- Strand IX: Global Connections

"A Vision of Powerful Teaching and Learning in the Social Studies." Silver Spring, Maryland: NCSS. 1994.

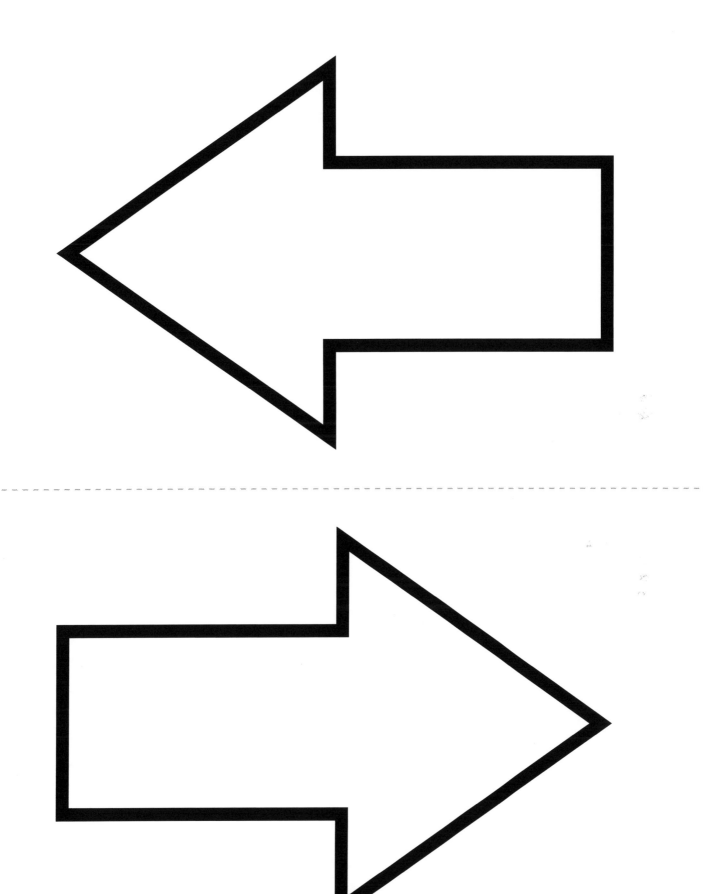

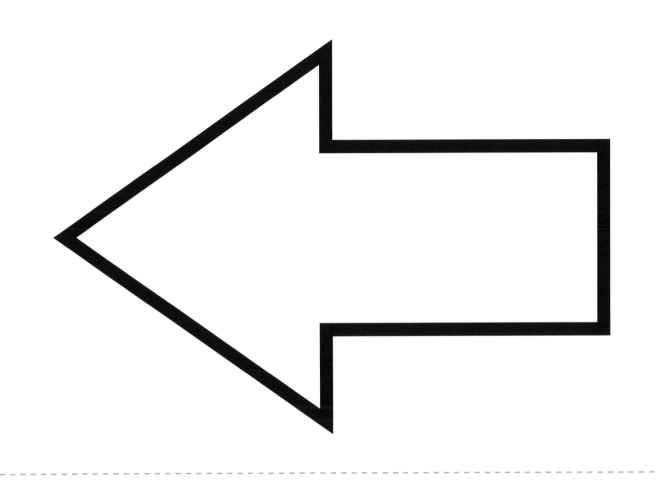

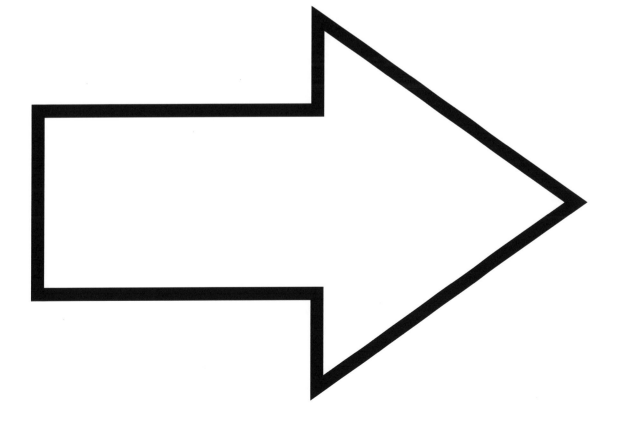

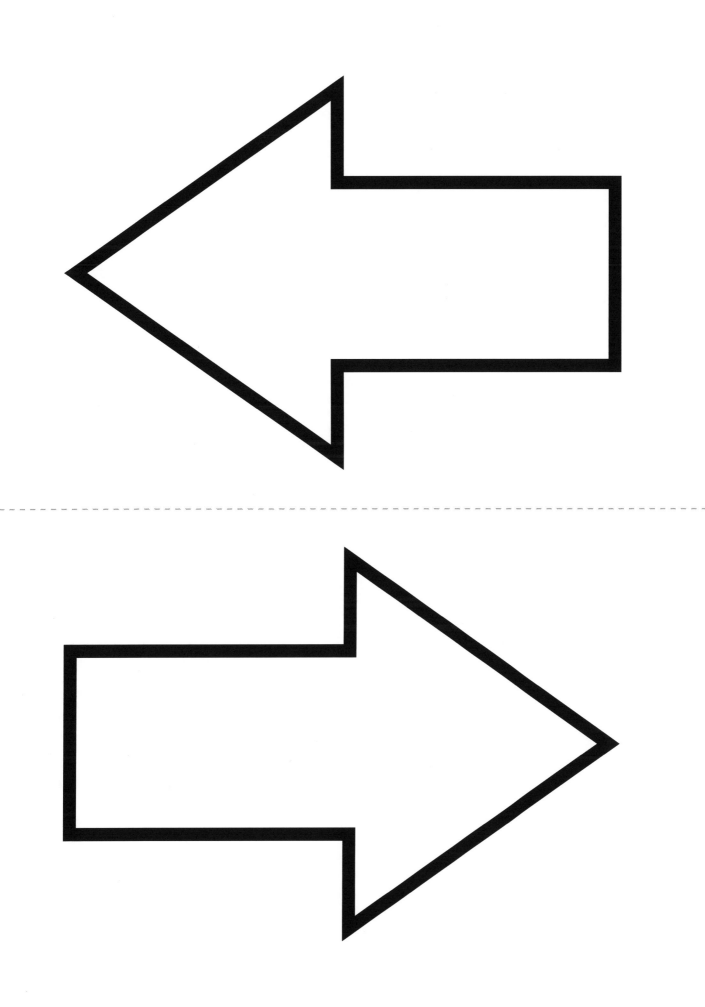

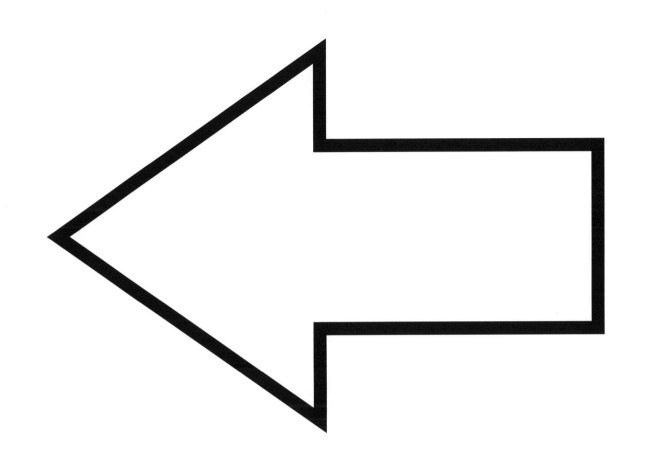
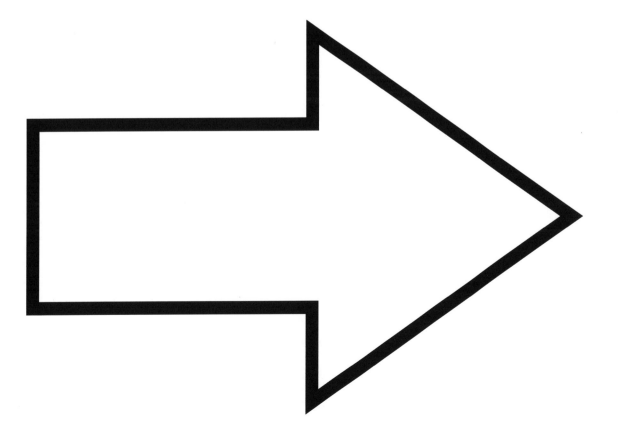

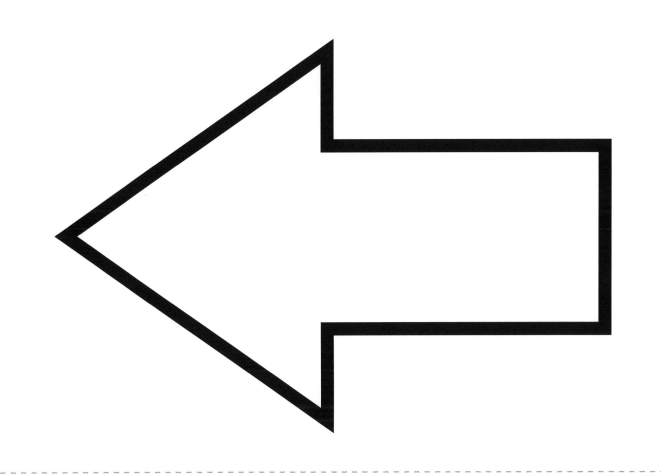
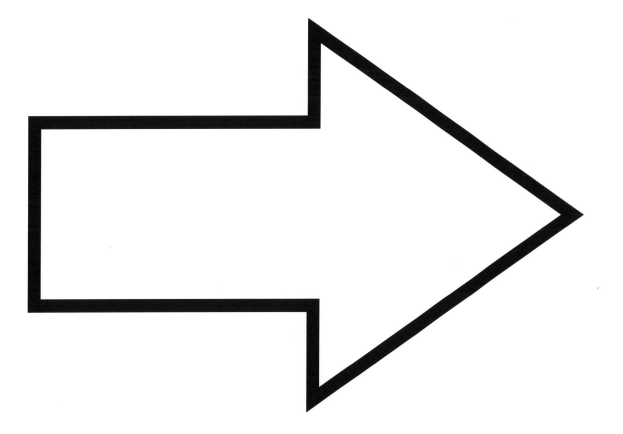

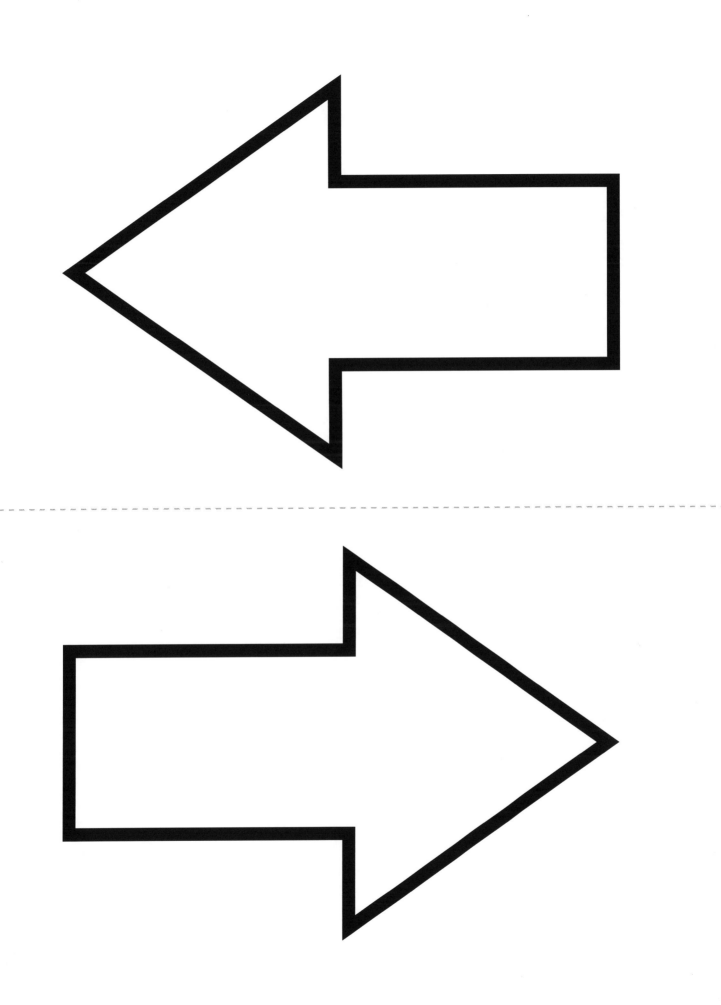

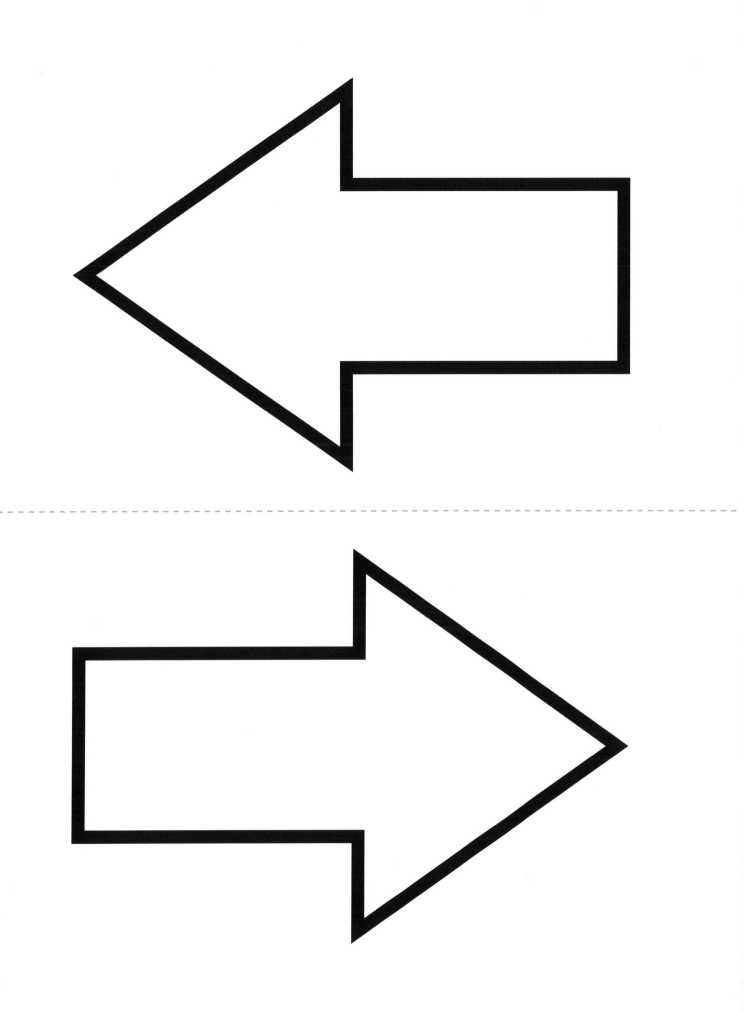

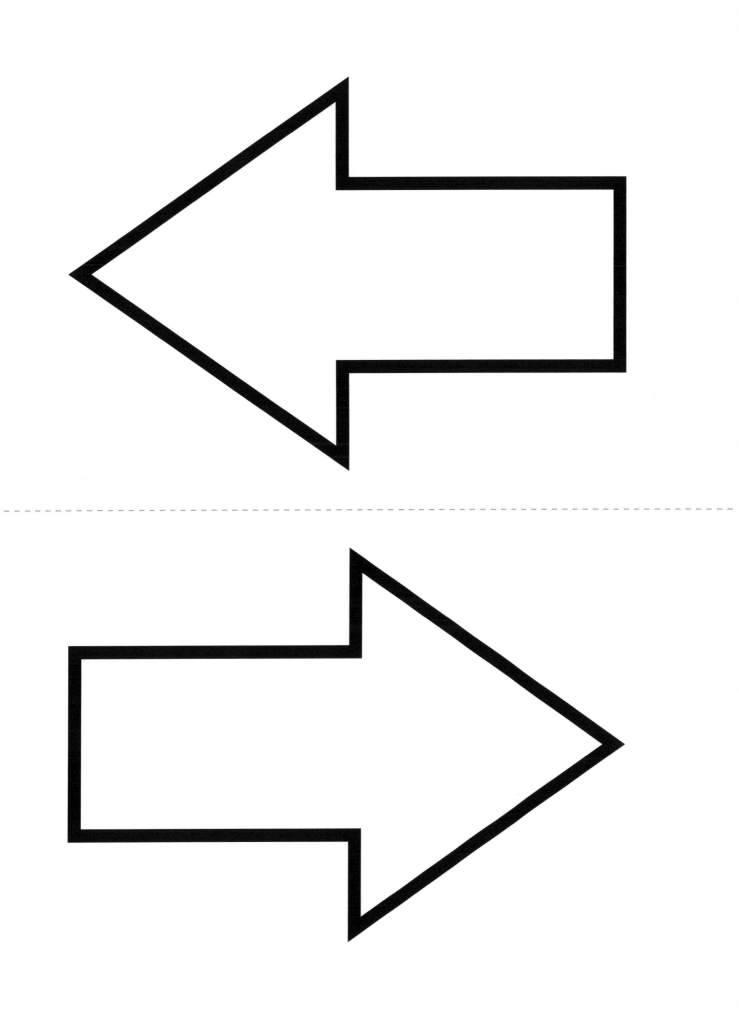

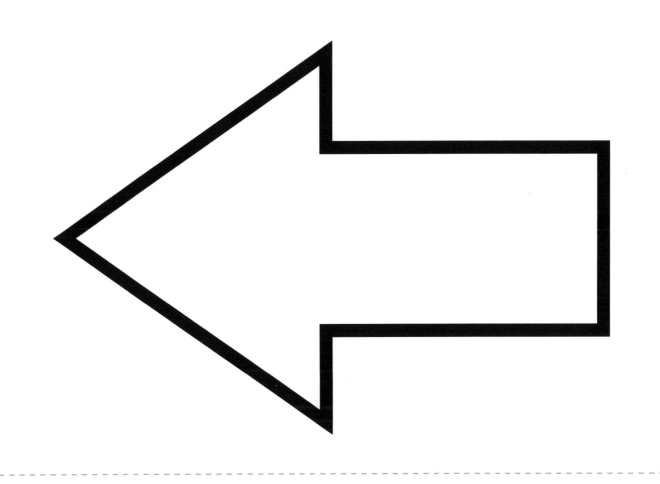

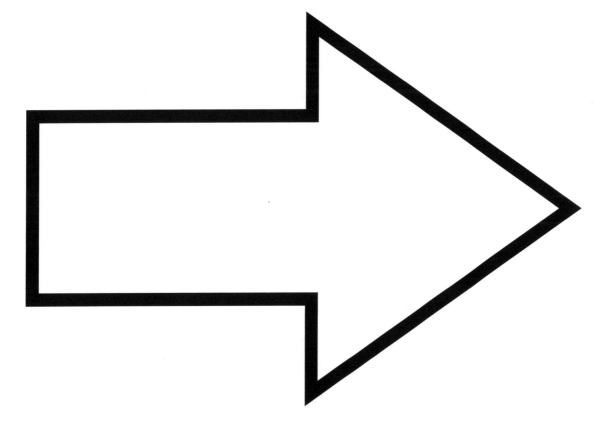

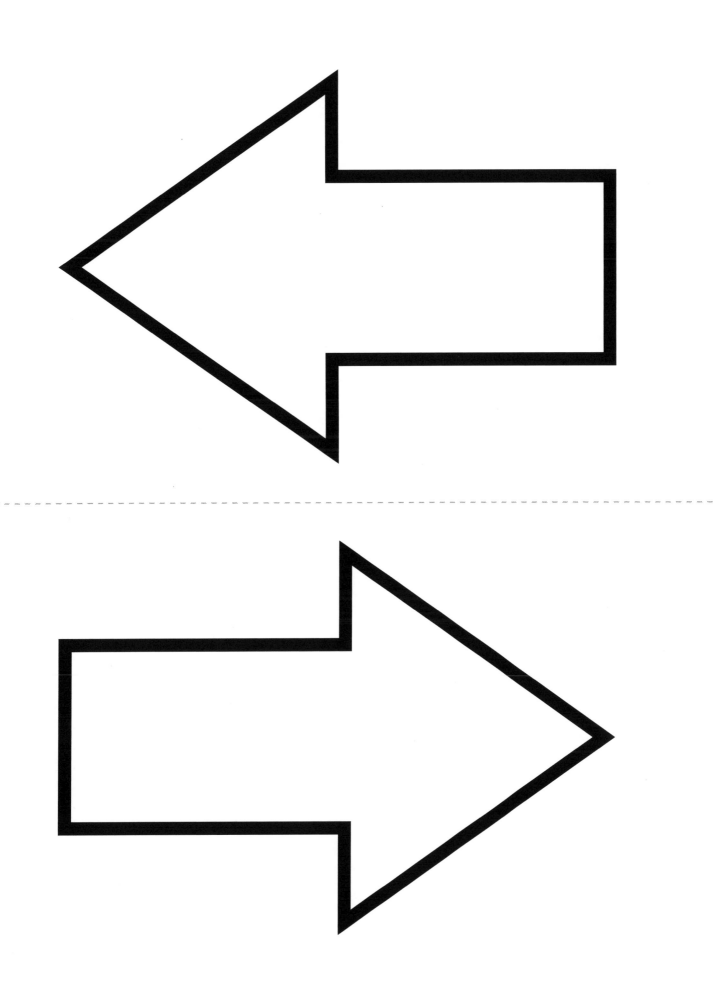

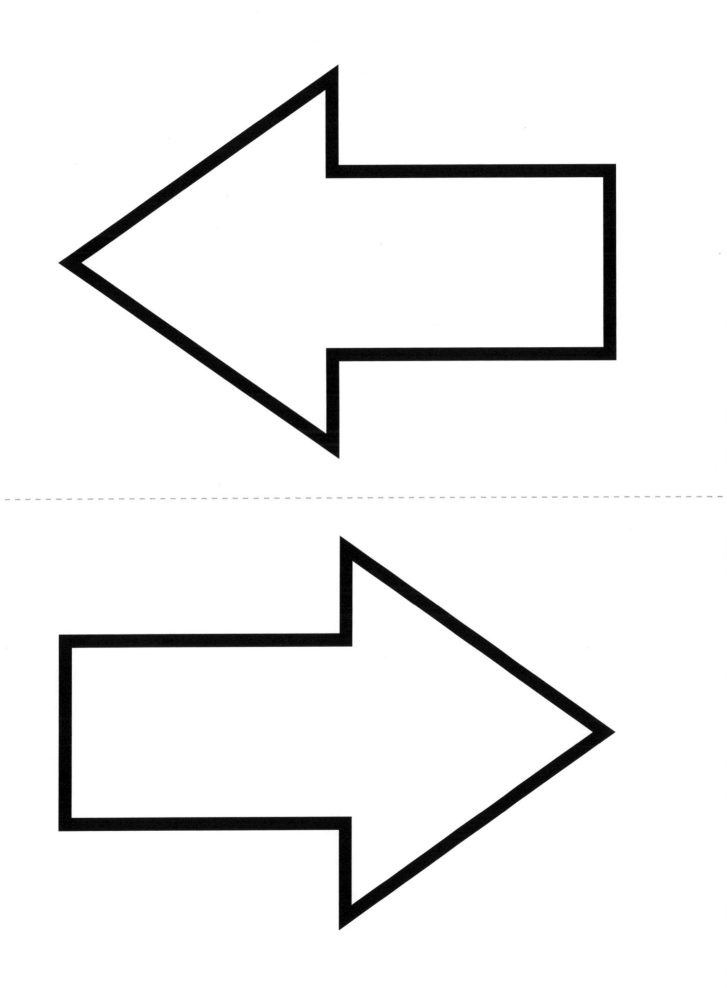

BEFORE HUMAN SETTLEMENT

ABOUT 50,000 YEARS AGO

BEFORE EUROPEAN CONTACT

1400

1425

1450

1475

1500

1525

1550

1575

1600

1625

1650

1675

1700

1725

1750

1775

1800

1825

1850

1875

INDUSTRY

AGRICULTURE

TRANSPORTATION & COMMUNICATION

Native American Issues

Women's Rights

Slavery & Abolitionism

UNIT 1　Discovery and Exploration　★ TEACHING NOTES ★

Prehistory — 1606

UNIT OVERVIEW

The story of America begins with the land. The geographical stage on which America's history has unfolded is the continent of North America. Thus, Activity Sheet 1-B— the first topic-specific activity in Unit 1 and in *The Giant American History Timeline 1*— focuses students' attention on the physical features of North America. Activity Sheet 1-A provides a unit overview.

The human history of North America began about 50,000 years ago. Around this time, an ice age lowered the sea level, exposing a land bridge. The Bering Strait land bridge, also called Beringia, connected North America, at its northwest extremity, to Asia. Groups of hunter-gatherers who were probably following animals crossed the land bridge and came to North America. Activity Sheet 1-C gives students an opportunity to map Beringia and the peopling of North America it facilitated.

People crossed the land bridge in countless cultural groupings over thousands of years. Over time, the people spread south, populating much of North America (and South America). They established territories and developed cultures, the latter of which are traditionally organized into culture areas, which students delineate and describe on Activity Sheet 1-D.

Now that the physical and human stage of North America has been set, students' attention is shifted to events on the other side of the globe—events that will lead to the European discovery of North America, European settlement, and in time, the birth of the United States.

Activity Sheet 1-E focuses on European trade with Asia, which led to the accidental European discovery of North America. Activity Sheet 1-F introduces students to the technology that made this trade, as well as the resulting explosion of European exploration, possible. Activity Sheets 1-G through 1-I focus on Christopher Columbus and the world-changing effects of his initial voyage to North America. Activity Sheets 1-J through 1-N guide students through the great age of European exploration, particularly the English, Spanish, and French explorations of North America, which led to the colonization discussed in Unit 2.

The Time Machine, Activity Sheet 1-O, compares the transportation people use today to the transportation used before Europeans came to North America. A Postcard From the Past, Activity Sheet 1-P, encourages students to learn about the Native Americans who once lived where the students' community now stands.

FOCUS ACTIVITIES

To focus the students' attention on this period of American history, consider the following activities:

North America Fun Facts

Share with the students remarkable facts about the physical geography of North America, or direct the students to consult an encyclopedia to locate such facts. Use these fun facts as a springboard into a discussion about North America as a setting for human activity. Discuss such things as natural resources, adaptation to various climates, and other aspects of the relationship between humans and their environment.

Journey by Sea

Remind the students that Europeans and Africans first came to North America by sea. Ask the students what it might have been like to sail across the Atlantic Ocean in a ship.

The Great Encounter

Have the students describe what they imagine a first meeting between European explorers and Native Americans might have been like. What did they think of each other? Why would they think these things? Have the students describe the encounter from each group's point of view.

CONSTRUCTING THE TIMELINE

This unit consists of 16 activity sheets that focus on significant events, people, and places related to the discovery and exploration of North America. Each activity sheet is designed to, once completed, become part of a posted classroom timeline of the period covered in the unit.

The Introduction (pages VII–XVI) provides a detailed explanation of how to use the activity sheets in the classroom and suggests various ways to construct the timeline using the completed activity sheets.

You can construct the timeline any way you see fit. Use the Timeline Components (pages XVIII–XXVI) to connect the activity sheets. Below are two possible timelines, constructed from the activity sheets in this unit and the Timeline Components.

Option 1: Basic Timeline

Construct this timeline to identify only the essential elements of the period.

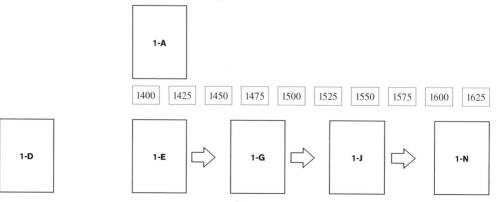

Option 2: Complete Timeline

Construct this timeline to identify the essential elements of the period, examine them in greater detail, and extend student learning.

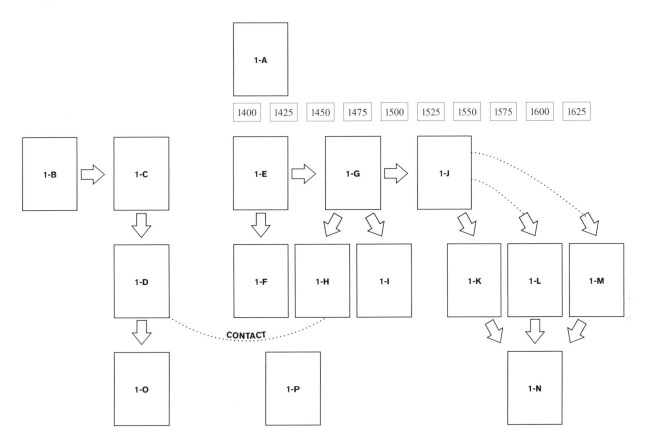

CRITICAL THINKING SKILLS

The activity sheets in this unit address various critical thinking skills. In addition, the constructed timeline emphasizes the essential critical thinking skills of identifying main ideas and details, sequencing events, and relating causes and effects.

Identifying Main Ideas and Details

Make sure the students understand the concepts of main idea and details. Explain that a main idea is a broad topic while details provide specific information about the main idea. Point out that Activity Sheet 1-A outlines the main ideas of the unit. Explain that the other activity sheets in the unit reflect the main ideas of the historical period the students are studying. Further explain that some activity sheets focus on the details related to specific topics.

As you and the students construct the timeline, show them that Activity Sheet 1-G forms a main idea and Activity Sheets 1-H and 1-I focus on details. Point out the similar relationship among Activity Sheet 1-J (main idea) and Activity Sheets 1-K, 1-L, and 1-M (details). Have the students annotate the Timeline Arrows appropriately. Challenge the students to find similar relationships or create them by rearranging the activity sheets.

Sequencing Events

Point out that the activity sheets that make up the timeline are sequential. Show the students how the Timeline Dates provide a concrete reference for when events happened and how they relate to other events. For example, Christopher Columbus discovered America in 1492 before John Cabot explored America in 1497. Make sure the students see that the Timeline Arrows indicate a chronological flow from left to right.

Relating Causes and Effects

Explain the relationship between a cause and an effect. Point out that there can be multiple causes and/or multiple effects in any situation.

As you and the students construct the timeline, show them that Activity Sheet 1-C focuses on the cause of the effect addressed on Activity Sheet 1-D. Point out that Activity Sheets 1-E and 1-F discuss the causes of the effect described on Activity Sheet 1-G. These events become the cause of the effects explained on Activity Sheets 1-H and 1-J. Activity Sheets 1-K, 1-L, and 1-M focus on the causes of the effects discussed on Activity Sheet 1-N. Have the students annotate the Timeline Arrows appropriately. Challenge the students to find similar relationships or create them by rearranging the activity sheets.

INDIVIDUAL ACTIVITY SHEET NOTES

The notes below provide a variety of tips on how to guide the students through the completion and extension of each activity sheet.

1-A. Discovery and Exploration

This activity is most appropriate for the students to complete with partners, in small groups, or as a whole class. For example, you might want to complete the questions with the whole class at the beginning of the unit and then have the students answer the questions at the end of the unit. Encourage the students to think of additional questions related to the topic. Before the students complete this activity, explain that the term "prehistory" refers to the period of time before history was first recorded.

1-B. Map Study: North America

Emphasize the idea that North America is the "stage" on which the "drama" of American history has unfolded. Guide the students in locating and labeling the major land and water features of North America.

1-C. The First Americans

Challenge the students to come up with reasons that prehistoric humans might have traveled. Were they just following animals for food? Or could they have also been curious about what they might find in other lands?

1-D. Native American Culture Areas

Explain that the first people who lived in North America were not just one group of people called Indians. Tell the students that there were thousands of distinct groups of people (often called Native Americans) and that each group had its own culture. Explain that the term "culture area" is used to help the students see the big picture of human settlement and recognize the wide variety of cultures in North America.

1-E. European Trade With Asia

Make sure the students understand that this trade led to the accidental European discovery of North America.

1-F. The Explorers' Ship

Explain that the ship shown is not a specific ship but that it represents the type of ship commonly used by explorers during this time period. Point out that this was the most impressive technology at that time. Tell the students that the carrack could sail anywhere in the world.

1-G. Biography: Christopher Columbus

Point out that the famous voyage of 1492 was the first of four voyages Columbus led to the "New World." On his last voyage, Columbus brought his 13-year-old son, Ferdinand. In fact, one-third of the sailors on that voyage were teenage boys.

1-H. The Columbian Exchange

Explain that the Columbian Exchange is still going on today. Point out that many of the things exchanged were diseases. The fact that Native Americans had no immunity to the diseases the Europeans brought with them is a major factor in the destruction of the Native American populations after European contact—many Native Americans died (or were killed) within a few years of Columbus's first voyage.

1-I. A Voice From the Past: Christopher Columbus

Discuss the assumptions made in this passage.

1-J. Exploring North America

Help the students understand how important Columbus's discovery was to the Europeans at that time. This was truly a "New World" to the Europeans, and the discovery generated tremendous excitement. Ask the students how they would feel if they just found out that life had been discovered on another planet. Explain that the Europeans probably felt the same kind of excitement when they discovered this new land. Tell the students that the European discovery of North America, and the exploration that followed, is one of the most important events in all of human history.

1-K. Cabot Explores North America for England

Remind the students that John Cabot's expedition is presented as a representative of many English explorations in North America. Others are identified on Activity Sheet 1-J. Consider having the students write their paragraphs in the form of encyclopedia entries or lessons for younger students.

1-L. Coronado Explores North America for Spain

Remind the students that Francisco de Coronado's expedition is presented as a representative of many Spanish explorations in North America. Others are identified on Activity Sheet 1-J. Consider having the students write their paragraphs in the form of encyclopedia entries or lessons for younger students.

1-M. Champlain Explores North America for France

Remind the students that Samuel de Champlain's expedition is presented as a representative of many French explorations in North America. Others are identified on Activity Sheet 1-J. Consider having the students write their paragraphs in the form of encyclopedia entries or lessons for younger students.

1-N. European Claims in North America

Explain that this activity sheet summarizes the information presented on the previous activity sheets in the unit.

1-O. The Time Machine: Transportation

Help the students identify the main points of the essay, which should be written in the left-hand circle of the Venn diagram. Emphasize the creative, appropriate, and often ingenious ways the Native Americans adapted to the different environments of North America. You might want to have the students locate photographs and/or illustrations of the various forms of transportation.

1-P. A Postcard From the Past: Native Americans in Your Community

Suggest that the students create postcards from a local museum or cultural center.

Discovery and Exploration

In the box below, draw a picture or attach a picture from a magazine or the Internet that represents this period of American history. The picture can be of anything you think is appropriate.

Ask questions about this period of American history. Then, answer them.

Question: WHO _____?

Answer: _____

Question: WHAT _____?

Answer: _____

Question: WHERE _____?

Answer: _____

Question: WHEN _____?

Answer: _____

Question: WHY _____?

Answer: _____

Question: HOW _____?

Answer: _____

This important date in American history is brought to you by

_____

North America

Label the major physical features of North America on the map below.
Then, use colored pencils to shade different features and regions of the continent.

This important date in American history is brought to you by

_____

★50,000 Years Ago ★ The First Americans

First, label the following items on the map below: North America, Asia, the Bering Strait, the Bering Sea, the Pacific Ocean, and the Arctic Ocean. Second, sketch Beringia on the map and label it. Third, draw arrows to represent human movement from Asia into North America. Finish by coloring the map and giving it an appropriate title.

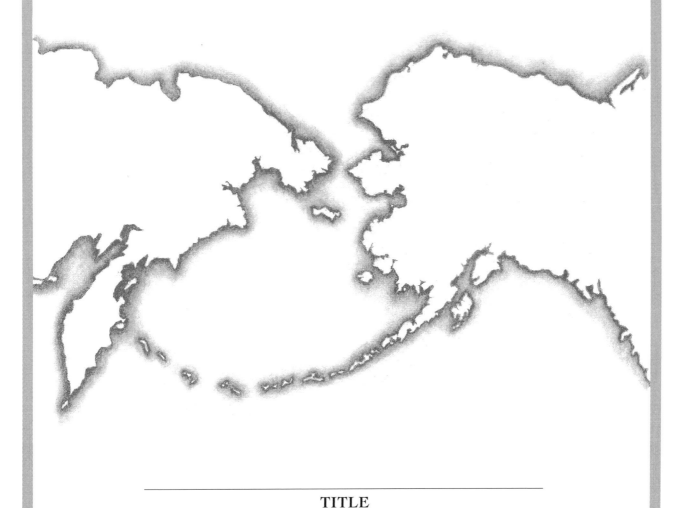

_____

TITLE

This important date in American history is brought to you by

_____

★ Before European Contact ★

Native American Culture Areas

Outline and label Native American culture areas on the map below. Use colored pencils to shade each area a different color. Then, draw a picture or write a few terms under each label to represent the culture area.

This important date in American history is brought to you by

_____

Answer the questions below.

Europe

Asia

WHY...

did the Europeans want to trade with Asia? _____

did the Europeans want to find a sea route to Asia? _____

WHAT...

was traded between Europe and Asia? _____

was the first sea route between Europe and Asia? _____

WHO...

in Portugal sponsored many trips to find a sea route? _____

was the first European explorer to reach Asia by sea? _____

WHEN...

did trade between Europe and Asia begin? _____

did this trade by sea begin? _____

HOW...

did Columbus hope to shorten the sea route to Asia? _____

_____

did European trade with Asia lead to the European discovery
of North America? _____

This important date in American history is brought to you by

_____

The type of ship called a carrack was one of the workhorses of European explorers during the 1400s and 1500s. Answer the questions below to see why.

The carrack had a triangular sail called a lateen. How did this help the ship?

_____

Some of the sails were rectangular. What do you think they were used for?

_____

The hold was deep and wide. Why would this be important on a long voyage?

_____

The hull had smooth sides. Why would this be an advantage on a ship?

_____

The rudder was large. Why would shipbuilders make it so big?

_____

The structures at the front (bow) and rear (stern) were called the forecastle and the

sterncastle. What were they used for? _____

_____

This important date in American history is brought to you by

_____

Left margin timeline: 1400, 1420, 1440, 1460, 1480, 1500, 1520, 1540, 1560, 1580, 1600

Right margin timeline: 1600, 1580, 1560, 1540, 1520, 1500, 1480, 1460, 1440, 1420, 1400

Answer the questions below.

T<small>HE</small> M<small>AN</small>

When did he live? _____

What was his nationality? _____

What words would you use to describe him?

_____

_____

H<small>IS</small> **1492** V<small>OYAGE</small>

What nation did Columbus sail for? _____

What were the names of his three ships? _____

_____

What was the purpose of his voyage? _____

_____

Why do we say he discovered America? _____

_____

Why might we say he discovered America by accident? _____

_____

Why do we sometimes call Native Americans "Indians"? _____

_____

This important date in American history is brought to you by

_____

The Columbian Exchange

Complete the definition below. Then, fill in the missing information in the chart. Use colored pencils to color the maps.

The Columbian Exchange is _____

_____

THE COLUMBIAN EXCHANGE

From the Americas to Europe	From Europe to the Americas
Plants	
Animals	
Other	

This important date in American history is brought to you by

_____

Christopher Columbus's discovery shocked the Europeans. The land he found seemed like a "New World" to them. The amazing and beautiful land was filled with plants and animals they had never seen or heard of. Many different kinds of people lived there as well. Christopher Columbus met one group of people when he first landed in America.

Read what Columbus wrote about the people he met. Then, answer the questions below.

> "They are always smiling…[their] speech is the
> sweetest and gentlest in the world…they are
> a loving people, without [greed]…weapons
> they have none…it appears that the people
> are [intelligent] and would be good servants."

Did Columbus think these people were his equals? How can you tell? _____

_____

_____

Do you think Columbus's view, or any part of it, might have become the typical way

Europeans viewed Native Americans? Explain your answer. _____

_____

What do you think of Columbus's statements? _____

_____

_____

This important date in American history is brought to you by

_____

★ The Century After Columbus ★

Exploring North America

Many explorers soon followed in Columbus's footsteps. Europeans explored more and more of North America.

The chart below lists some of the most important explorers of this time period. Fill in the missing information. Then, answer the question below.

Explorer	Country or Countries Explored For	Date of Journey or Journeys	Area Explored
John Cabot			
Amerigo Vespucci			
Vasco Núñez de Balboa			
Juan Ponce de León			
Giovanni da Verrazano			
Sebastian Cabot			
Jacques Cartier			
Hernando de Soto			
Francisco Vasquez de Coronado			
Sir Martin Frobisher			
Juan de Oñate			
Samuel de Champlain			

How is Amerigo Vespucci's name still with us today? _____

_____

_____

This important date in American history is brought to you by

_____

★1497★ Cabot Explores North America for England

England sent many explorers to North America. These adventurers claimed parts of North America for England. One of the most important explorers was John Cabot.

Trace Cabot's route on the map below. Use colored pencils to color the map. Then, write a paragraph that tells about Cabot and his exploration of North America.

This important date in American history is brought to you by

_____

Spain sent many explorers to North America. These adventurers claimed parts of North America for Spain. One of the most important explorers was Francisco Vasquez de Coronado.

Trace Coronado's route on the map below. Use colored pencils to color the map. Then, write a paragraph that tells about Coronado and his exploration of North America.

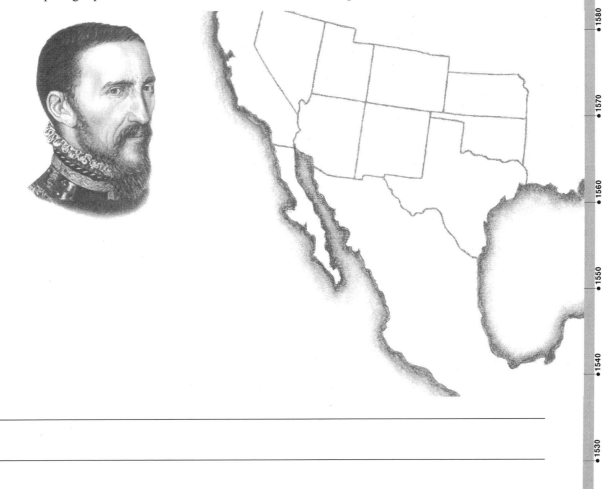

This important date in American history is brought to you by

★1603★ Champlain Explores North America for France

France sent many explorers to North America. These adventurers claimed parts of North America for France. One of the most important explorers was Samuel de Champlain.

Trace Champlain's route on the map below. Use colored pencils to color the map. Then, write a paragraph that tells about Champlain and his exploration of North America.

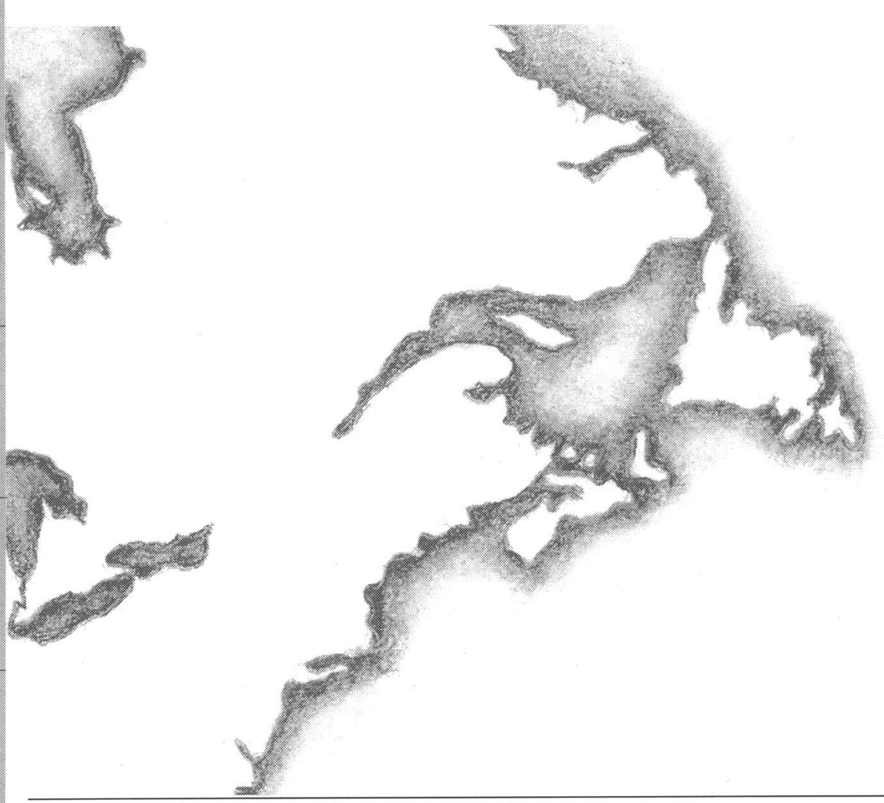

____

____

____

____

____

____

This important date in American history is brought to you by

____

By 1606, England, Spain, and France had claimed much of North America for themselves.

Label the map below to show the area each country claimed. Use colored pencils to shade each country's claims a different color.

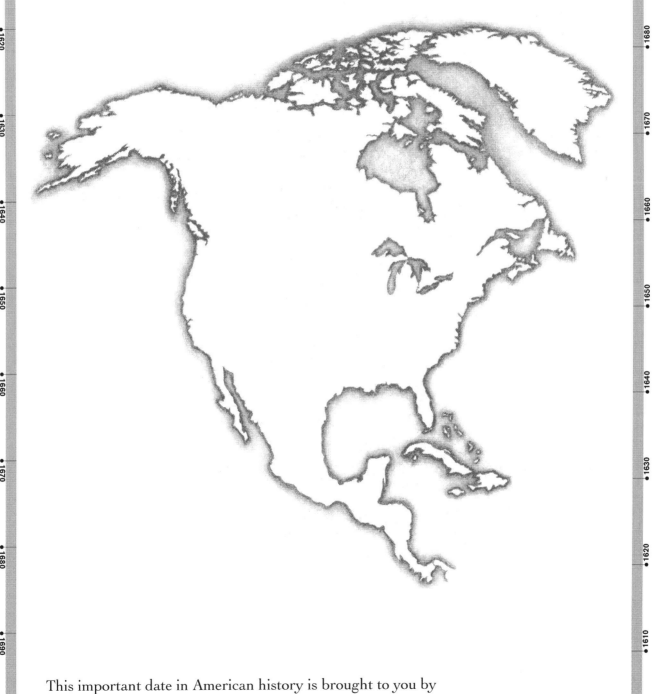

This important date in American history is brought to you by

_____

Activate the Time Machine to learn about transportation in North America before the Europeans arrived. In the left-hand circle, write facts about the Native Americans' transportation during that time. In the right-hand circle, write facts about transportation today. In the space where the circles overlap, write facts about transportation that both time periods have in common.

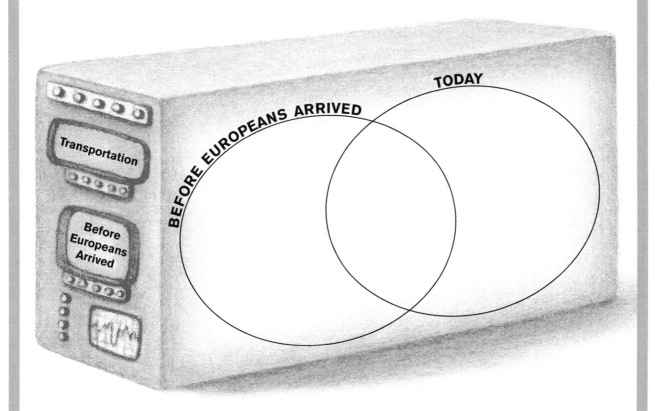

Native Americans did not have horses until they were brought to North America by Europeans. Still, Native Americans developed many methods of transportation.

Mostly, they traveled by foot. Sometimes, they walked great distances to trade things. Native Americans walked along trails they had made. These trails criss-crossed North America. Some of the trails stretched for hundreds of miles!

Native Americans were also experts at using North America's lakes and streams to travel. The Native Americans built a wide variety of boats, including canoes, dugouts, bullboats, and kayaks.

In the cold north, Native Americans used dogsleds, toboggans, and snowshoes to make travel over ice and snow easier.

This important trip into American history is brought to you by

_____

★ Native Americans in Your Community ★

Native Americans lived all over North America. Which Native American culture lived closest to the community you live in now? Conduct research to find out.

Use the Internet or any other resources your teacher suggests. Read the articles, and study the illustrations. When you have gathered enough information, make a postcard.

On the front of the postcard, draw a picture or attach a picture from a magazine or the Internet that gives some information about the first Americans to live in your area. On the back of the postcard, write a caption that explains the picture. Then, write a note to a friend that tells something about how these people lived.

POST CARD

PLACE
STAMP
HERE

NAME AND ADDRESS HERE

This important place in American history is brought to you by

UNIT 2 Colonial America

1585–1776

UNIT OVERVIEW

The English colonial period in American history truly began in 1607. At this time, the first permanent English settlement in America, Jamestown, was established. Earlier attempts, including the one at Roanoke, which was first settled in 1585, failed, but the settlers blazed the trail. The period of colonial America ended in 1776 when the 13 English colonies that had been established declared their independence from England. This unit provides a general overview of the colonial period. Unit 3 specifically covers the late colonial period, marked by colonial unrest.

The colonial period is one of the most important periods in American history. Much of our national character was forged during this time. Many of our most treasured national memories are from this period. The tale of John Smith and Pocahontas is an enduring favorite. The "Lost Colony" of Roanoke Island is one of our great mysteries. We still celebrate Thanksgiving, a tradition started by the Pilgrims. The activity sheets in this unit introduce the students to such important stories, as well as the other significant events of the period.

Activity Sheet 2-A provides a unit overview. Activity Sheets 2-B through 2-G focus on the three primary early settlements: Roanoke, Jamestown, and Plymouth. Activity Sheet 2-H sets the geographical stage in the form of a map, while Activity Sheets 2-I through 2-K provide the students with an opportunity to share what they know about each colony. Activity Sheet 2-L is about the French and Indian War, through which England solidified its possession of North America. Activity Sheet 2-M hints at the coming revolution with a graphic depiction of the results of the Quartering Act.

The Time Machine, Activity Sheet 2-N, compares education today to education during the colonial period. A Postcard From the Past, Activity Sheet 2-O, is about Colonial Williamsburg.

FOCUS ACTIVITIES

To focus the students' attention on this period of American history, consider the following activities:

A Different World

Have the students identify things that are part of their world but that did not exist during the colonial period (for example, telephones, automobiles, and antibiotics). Record their responses on the board. Then, have the class divide the items into categories (for example, communication, transportation, and medicine). Explain that there were major differences to nearly all aspects of colonial life. Then, challenge the students to think of ways colonial life was similar to their lives today.

Thanksgiving

Ask the students to share what they know about the first Thanksgiving. Discuss possible motives the Pilgrims had in settling Plymouth. Talk about what their lives were like in Plymouth. Explain that this lifestyle was typical of all the colonies during the colonial period.

Great Mysteries

Have the students identify some great unsolved mysteries (for example, the fate of Amelia Earhart and whether or not the Loch Ness monster really exists). Tell the students that one of the greatest mysteries in American history is the story of the "Lost Colony." Summarize the story, or ask a student volunteer to tell the story. Then, discuss possible solutions to the mystery.

CONSTRUCTING THE TIMELINE

This unit consists of 15 activity sheets that focus on significant events, people, and places related to colonial America. Each activity sheet is designed to, once completed, become part of a posted classroom timeline of the period covered in the unit.

The Introduction (pages VII–XVI) provides a detailed explanation of how to use the activity sheets in the classroom and suggests various ways to construct the timeline using the completed activity sheets.

You can construct the timeline any way you see fit. Use the Timeline Components (pages XVIII–XXVI) to connect the activity sheets. Below are two possible timelines, constructed from the activity sheets in this unit and the Timeline Components.

Option 1: Basic Timeline

Construct this timeline to identify only the essential elements of the period.

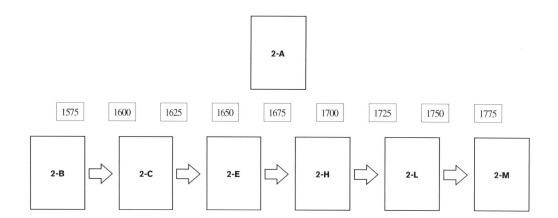

Option 2: Complete Timeline

Construct this timeline to identify the essential elements of the period, examine them in greater detail, and extend student learning.

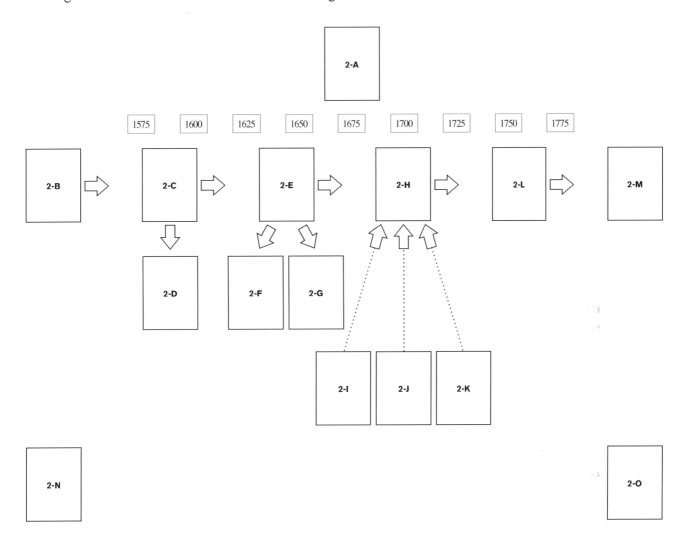

CRITICAL THINKING SKILLS

The activity sheets in this unit address various critical thinking skills. In addition, the constructed timeline emphasizes the essential critical thinking skills of identifying main ideas and details, sequencing events, and relating causes and effects.

Identifying Main Ideas and Details

Point out that Activity Sheet 2-A outlines the main ideas of the unit. Explain that the topics of the other activity sheets in the unit reflect the main ideas of the historical period the students are studying. Further explain that some activity sheets focus on the details related to specific topics.

As you and the students construct the timeline, show them that the following activity sheets form main idea/detail relationships: 2-C/2-D; 2-E/2-F and 2-G; 2-H/2-I, 2-J, and 2-K. Have the students annotate the Timeline Arrows appropriately. Challenge the students to find similar relationships or create them by rearranging the activity sheets.

Sequencing Events

Point out that the activity sheets that make up the timeline are sequential. Show the students how the Timeline Dates provide a concrete reference for when events happened and how they relate to other events. For example, Jamestown was settled in 1607 before the Pilgrims sailed to America in 1620. Make sure the students see that the Timeline Arrows indicate a chronological flow from left to right.

Relating Causes and Effects

Review the relationship between a cause and an effect. Remind the students that there can be multiple causes and/or multiple effects in any situation.

As you and the students construct the timeline, show them that Activity Sheet 2-L focuses on the cause of the effect addressed on Activity Sheet 2-M. Have the students annotate the Timeline Arrows appropriately. Challenge the students to find similar relationships or create them by rearranging the activity sheets.

INDIVIDUAL ACTIVITY SHEET NOTES

The notes below provide a variety of tips on how to guide the students through the completion and extension of each activity sheet.

2-A. Colonial America

This activity is most appropriate for the students to complete with partners, in small groups, or as a whole class. For example, you might want to complete the questions with the whole class at the beginning of the unit and then have the students answer the questions at the end of the unit. Encourage the students to think of additional questions related to the topic.

2-B. The Lost Colony

Discuss logical possibilities of what could have happened to the colonists who lived on Roanoke Island. Ask the students if they think any type of research could be done today that could solve the mystery.

2-C. Jamestown

Emphasize the importance of Jamestown as the first permanent English colony in America and therefore the origin of the United States. Point out the small size of the colony compared to the vast continent that was wilderness to the settlers.

2-D. Biography: John Smith and Pocahontas

Ask the students why the story of John Smith and Pocahontas is still such a popular story today.

2-E. The Pilgrims

The actual *Mayflower* was only about 90 feet long and 25 feet wide. You might want to take the students outside and help them create a life-size outline of the ship. Tell the students how crowded the ship was with 102 Puritans onboard and how dangerous the voyage across the Atlantic Ocean was.

2-F. A Voice From the Past: The *Mayflower* Compact

Explain that a compact is an agreement between two or more people. Have the students compare the *Mayflower* Compact to the kinds of legal agreements that people live by today, including the Constitution.

2-G. The First Thanksgiving

Ask the students if they think the illustration is an accurate depiction of the first Thanksgiving. Discuss how it is possible to illustrate things that occurred before photography was invented. Explain that people do a lot of research and make inferences in order to illustrate historical events that were not photographed.

2-H. Map Study: Colonial America

Activity Sheets 2-H through 2-K are dated 1733 because that is the year by which all 13 colonies had become permanently settled. Consider having the students shade the New England colonies, the middle colonies, and the southern colonies different colors.

2-I. The New England Colonies

Explain that the New England colonies were Plymouth, New Hampshire, Connecticut, and Rhode Island.

2-J. The Middle Colonies

Tell the students that the middle colonies were New York, Delaware, New Jersey, and Pennsylvania.

2-K. The Southern Colonies

Explain that the southern colonies were Virginia, Maryland, North Carolina, South Carolina, and Georgia.

2-L. The French and Indian War

Emphasize that the chief result of this conflict was the solidification of British control in North America.

2-M. The Quartering Act

Explain that this act was amended in 1774, making it even more intrusive. Discuss the relationship between the Quartering Act and the Third Amendment of the Constitution.

2-N. The Time Machine: Education

Help the students identify the main points of the essay, which should be written in the left-hand circle of the Venn diagram. You might want to have the students complete one of their regular assignments as if they are students in the colonial period. Ask each student to turn in a homemade "hornbook" that includes the assignment.

2-O. A Postcard From the Past: Visiting Colonial Williamsburg

Suggest that the students visit www.history.org to gather information about Colonial Williamsburg.

In the box below, draw a picture or attach a picture from a magazine or the Internet that represents this period of American history. The picture can be of anything you think is appropriate.

Ask questions about this period of American history. Then, answer them.

Question: WHO_____?

Answer:_____

Question: WHAT_____?

Answer:_____

Question: WHERE _____?

Answer:_____

Question: WHEN _____?

Answer:_____

Question: WHY_____?

Answer:_____

Question: HOW_____?

Answer:_____

This important date in American history is brought to you by

_____

What happened to the colonists of Roanoke Island? No one knows for sure. That is why we call it the "Lost Colony." The fate of the 118 people—men, women, and children—remains one of the great mysteries of American history.

Answer the questions below.

ROANOKE ISLAND

THE COLONY

Where was it located? _____

_____

What country established it? _____

_____

THE PEOPLE

How many colonists were there? _____

Who was their leader? _____

Who was Virginia Dare? _____

_____

THE MYSTERY

How was the word "CROATOAN" involved? _____

_____

What might have happened to the colonists? _____

_____

_____

This important date in American history is brought to you by

_____

Learn about Jamestown by completing the sentences below.

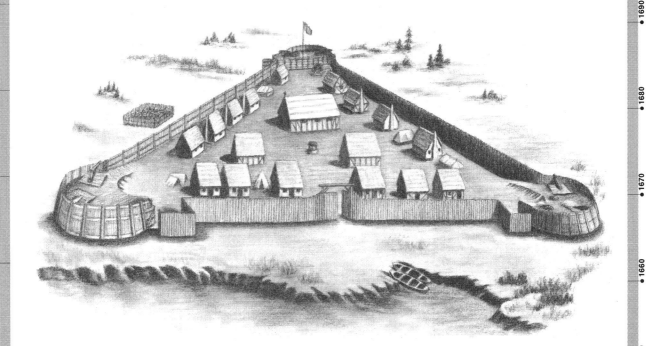

Jamestown was the first _____ English Settlement in North America.

Jamestown is located in what is now the state of _____.

Jamestown settlers hoped to find _____.

Jamestown' settlers began to grow _____, which helped the colony survive.

This important date in American history is brought to you by

_____

Answer the questions below.

JOHN SMITH

When did he live? _____

What was his nationality? _____

How did he help the Jamestown settlers survive?_____

_____

_____

What words would you use to describe John Smith? _____

_____

POCAHONTAS

When did she live?_____

What was her nationality?_____

How did she help the Jamestown settlers survive? _____

_____

_____

What words would you use to describe Pocahontas? _____

_____

How were John Smith and Pocahontas important to each other? _____

_____

This important date in American history is brought to you by

_____

★ 1620 ★ The Pilgrims

Answer the questions below.

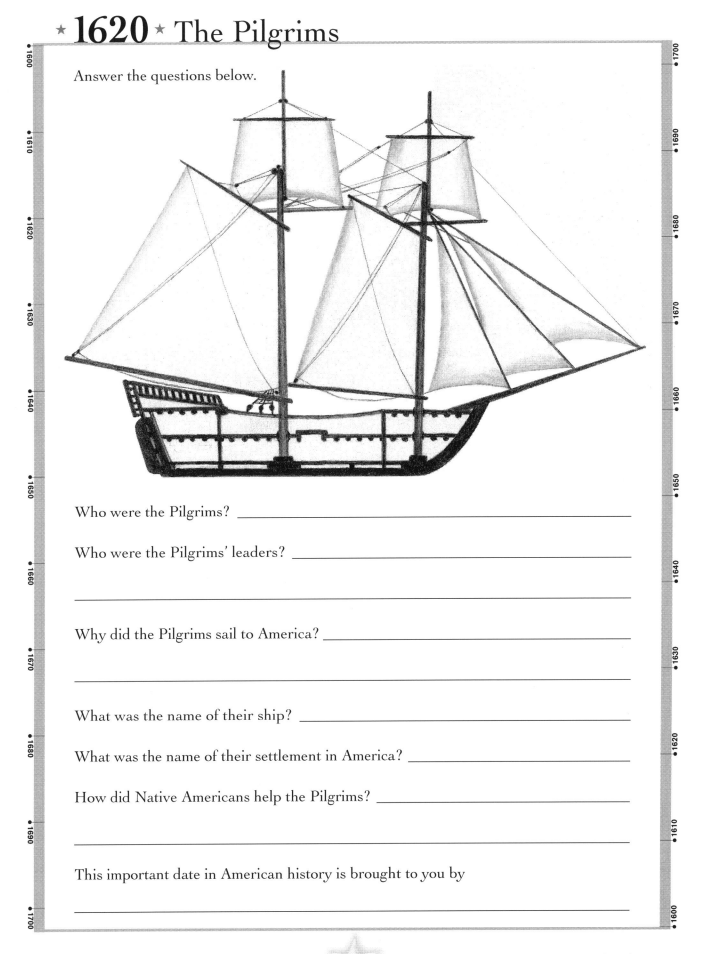

Who were the Pilgrims? _____

Who were the Pilgrims' leaders? _____

_____

Why did the Pilgrims sail to America? _____

_____

What was the name of their ship? _____

What was the name of their settlement in America? _____

How did Native Americans help the Pilgrims? _____

_____

This important date in American history is brought to you by

_____

1600 • 1610 • 1620 • 1630 • 1640 • 1650 • 1660 • 1670 • 1680 • 1690 • 1700

1700 • 1690 • 1680 • 1670 • 1660 • 1650 • 1640 • 1630 • 1620 • 1610 • 1600

The Mayflower Compact

The Pilgrims were afraid that their group would break up. To keep themselves together, they wrote an agreement, or a compact. It was called the Mayflower Compact.

Read the section of the Mayflower Compact below. Then, answer the questions.

FROM THE MAYFLOWER COMPACT:

"We…combine ourselves together…for our better Ordering and Preservation…and…to [make] just and equal Laws…as shall be thought most [fitting] and convenient for the general Good…unto which we promise… Obedience."

What does this section of the Mayflower Compact mean? Rewrite it in your own words.

_____

_____

_____

_____

Why did the Pilgrims need laws? _____

_____

This important date in American history is brought to you by

_____

Answer the questions below.

Why did the Pilgrims have a feast? _____

_____

What did the Pilgrims feel thankful for? _____

_____

Study the picture above. What conclusions can you draw about how the Pilgrims lived?

Explain your answer. _____

_____

Today, we celebrate Thanksgiving every November. Why do you think we have this

holiday? _____

_____

This important date in American history is brought to you by

_____

Timeline marks (left): 1600, 1610, 1620, 1630, 1640, 1650, 1660, 1670, 1680, 1690, 1700

Timeline marks (right): 1700, 1690, 1680, 1670, 1660, 1650, 1640, 1630, 1620, 1610, 1600

Label and shade the following items on the map below: the 13 colonies, major bodies of water, and the Appalachian Mountains. Then, outline, label, and shade the British, French, and Spanish claims.

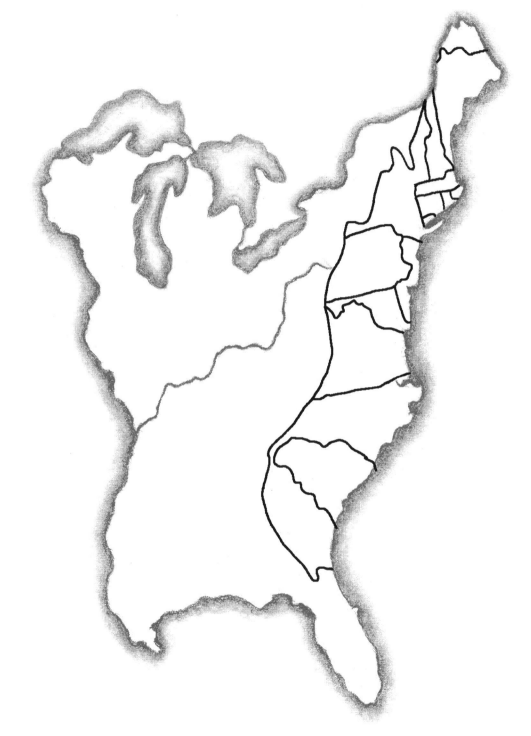

This important date in American history is brought to you by

_____

Shade the New England Colonies on the map. Then, complete the chart and answer the questions below.

THE NEW ENGLAND COLONIES

Colony	Date Settled	Reason(s) for Settlement	Main Economic Activities

Which colony was established by the Pilgrims? _____

Which colony was established by people fleeing another colony? _____

Why were ships important to the economy of the New England colonies? _____

_____

_____

This important date in American history is brought to you by

_____

★ 1733 ★ The Middle Colonies

Shade the Middle Colonies on the map. Then, complete the chart and answer the questions below.

THE MIDDLE COLONIES

Colony	Date Settled	Reason(s) for Settlement	Main Economic Activities

Which middle colony was established by Quakers? _____

What were the two main economic activities in the middle colonies? _____

_____

_____

This important date in American history is brought to you by _____

_____

Shade the Southern Colonies on the map. Then, complete the chart and answer the questions below.

THE SOUTHERN COLONIES

Colony	Date Settled	Reason(s) for Settlement	Main Economic Activities

Which southern colony was the site of the first permanent English settlement in

America? _____

What was the most important crop in the southern colonies? _____

Which southern colony was established for religious reasons? _____

This important date in American history is brought to you by

_____

Answer the questions below.

Who fought in the French and Indian War? _____

_____

Who won the war? _____

What was the most important effect of the war? _____

_____

_____

_____

This important date in American history is brought to you by

_____

Study the illustration below. Then, complete the writing activities.

Imagine that you are one of the colonists. Write a sentence that describes this scene. Then, explain why you oppose the Quartering Act.

_____

_____

_____

Imagine that you are one of the soldiers. Write a sentence that describes this scene. Then, explain why you support the Quartering Act.

_____

_____

_____

This important date in American history is brought to you by

_____

Activate the Time Machine to learn about education in North America during the colonial period. In the left-hand circle, write facts about education during that time. In the right-hand circle, write facts about education today. In the space where the circles overlap, write facts about education that both time periods have in common.

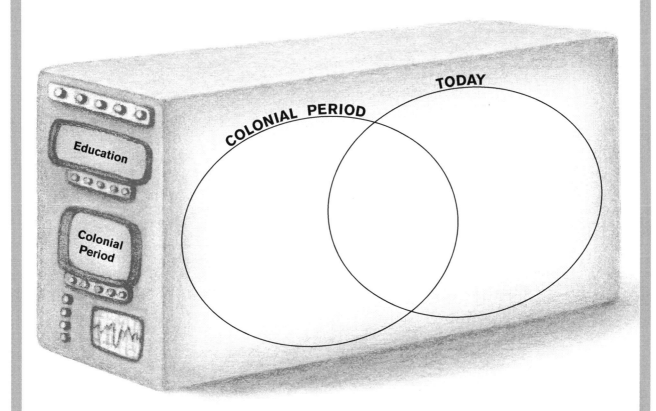

In colonial days, poor children were educated at home. They were taught by their parents and other older relatives. Boys and girls learned different things. Boys learned such things as how to plant and grow crops. Girls learned such things as how to sew and cook. Both boys and girls learned about religion. Some learned how to read and write.

Wealthy children attended school or had private tutors. The schools were small. Many schools were in private homes. Students learned "the basics": how to read, how to write, and how to do arithmetic. Ideas from the Bible were usually taught and used to help students practice their reading and writing.

In schools, children used hornbooks. These were boards with paper attached to them. On the paper were written things for the children to learn and memorize, such as the alphabet.

This important trip into American history is brought to you by

_____

Every year, millions of people from all over the world visit Williamsburg, Virginia. Why do so many people travel so far? Conduct research to find out.

Use the Internet or any other resources your teacher suggests. Read the articles, and study the illustrations. When you have gathered enough information, make a postcard.

On the front of the postcard, draw a picture or attach a picture from a magazine or the Internet that gives some information about Williamsburg. On the back of the postcard, write a caption that explains the picture. Then, write a note to a friend that tells about things to do and see in Williamsburg.

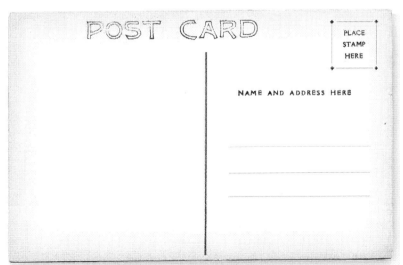

This important place in American history is brought to you by

UNIT 3 The Revolutionary Period   ★ TEACHING NOTES ★

1765—1783

UNIT OVERVIEW

The American Revolution, also called the Revolutionary War, began in 1775 with the shots fired at Lexington and Concord and lasted until 1783 when the Treaty of Paris was signed. The tensions that led to the American Revolution, however, began years earlier. Thus, this unit begins in 1765, soon after the French and Indian War ended.

Activity Sheet 3-A provides a unit overview, and Activity Sheet 3-B addresses the causes and effects of the infamous Sugar Act of 1764 and the Stamp Act of 1765. Activity Sheets 3-C through 3-F familiarize the students with the famous series of events—the enactment of the Townshend Acts, the Boston Massacre, the Boston Tea Party, and the enactment of the Intolerable Acts—that led to the calling of the First Continental Congress in 1774, addressed on Activity Sheet 3-G.

Activity Sheet 3-H focuses on the beginning of the American Revolution, the outbreak of fighting at Lexington and Concord, which led to the Second Continental Congress and the issuing of the Declaration of Independence. Activity Sheet 3-I features an excerpt from the Declaration of Independence. Students map the major battles of the conflict on Activity Sheet 3-J and research the life of George Washington, the "Father of Our Country," on Activity Sheet 3-K. Activity Sheet 3-L details the terms of the Treaty of Paris, which officially ended the conflict and helped define the new nation. Activity Sheet 3-M gives the students a visual understanding of how much land was gained because of the Treaty of Paris.

The Time Machine Activity, Activity Sheet 3-N, compares the food people eat today to the food people ate during the colonial period. A Postcard From the Past, Activity Sheet 3-O, is about Independence National Historic Park.

FOCUS ACTIVITIES

To focus the students' attention on this period of American history, consider the following activities:

Famous Phrases

Begin by writing several expressions and quotes associated with the American Revolution on the board (for example, "No taxation without representation," "Don't fire until you see the whites of their eyes," and "I regret that I have but one life to give for my country"). Continue adding items to the list until the students realize that all the items are related to the American Revolution. Then, discuss the meaning of each expression or quote.

First in War…

Invite the students to share what they know about George Washington. Help them sort the myths from the historical facts. Discuss George Washington as the "Father of Our Country" as well as a real, flesh-and-blood person.

Independence Day

Ask the students what important holiday we celebrate in July. Ask them why "Independence Day" is a more accurate name for this holiday than "The Fourth of July." Discuss whose independence we celebrate on July 4 and from whom independence was gained. Use this discussion as a way to gauge the students' knowledge about the American Revolution.

CONSTRUCTING THE TIMELINE

This unit consists of 15 activity sheets that focus on significant events, people, and places related to the American Revolution. Each activity sheet is designed to, once completed, become part of a posted classroom timeline of the period covered in the unit.

The Introduction (pages VII–XVI) provides a detailed explanation of how to use the activity sheets in the classroom and suggests various ways to construct the timeline using the completed activity sheets.

You can construct the timeline any way you see fit. Use the Timeline Components (pages XVIII–XXVI) to connect the activity sheets. Below are two possible timelines, constructed from the activity sheets in this unit and the Timeline Components.

Option 1: Basic Timeline

Construct this timeline to identify only the essential elements of the period.

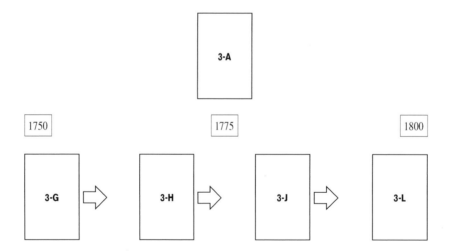

Option 2: Complete Timeline

Construct this timeline to identify the essential elements of the period, examine them in greater detail, and extend student learning.

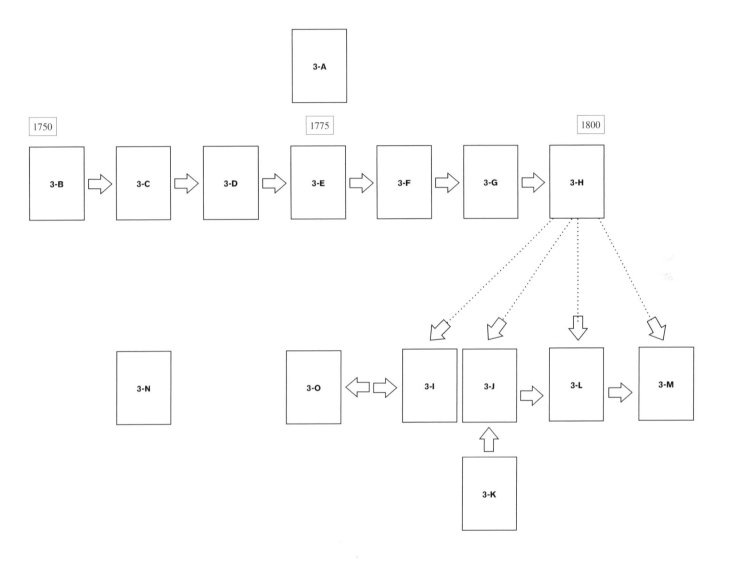

CRITICAL THINKING SKILLS

The activity sheets in this unit address various critical thinking skills. In addition, the constructed timeline emphasizes the essential critical thinking skills of identifying main ideas and details, sequencing events, and relating causes and effects.

Identifying Main Ideas and Details

Point out that Activity Sheet 3-A outlines the main ideas of the unit. Explain that the topics of the other activity sheets in the unit reflect the main ideas of the historical period the students are studying. Further explain that some activity sheets focus on the details related to specific topics.

As you and the students construct the timeline, show them that Activity Sheet 3-J forms a main idea and Activity Sheet 3-K focuses on details. Have the students annotate the Timeline Arrow appropriately. Challenge the students to find similar relationships or create them by rearranging the activity sheets.

Sequencing Events

Point out that the activity sheets that make up the timeline are sequential. Show the students how the Timeline Dates provide a concrete reference for when events happened and how they relate to other events. (For example, the Boston Massacre was in 1770 before the Boston Tea Party in 1773.) Make sure the students see that the Timeline Arrows indicate a chronological flow from left to right.

Relating Causes and Effects

As you and the students construct the timeline, show them that Activity Sheets 3-B through 3-H form a cause-and-effect chain. Point out that the cause discussed on Activity Sheet 3-J led to the effect described on Activity Sheet 3-L and thereby Activity Sheet 3-M. Have the students annotate the Timeline Arrows appropriately. Challenge the students to find similar relationships or create them by rearranging the activity sheets.

INDIVIDUAL ACTIVITY SHEET NOTES

The notes below provide a variety of tips on how to guide the students through the completion and extension of each activity sheet.

3-A. The Revolutionary Period

This activity is most appropriate for the students to complete with partners, in small groups, or as a whole class. For example, you might want to complete the questions with the whole class at the beginning of the unit and then have the students answer the questions at the end of the unit. Encourage the students to think of additional questions related to the topic.

3-B. "No Taxation Without Representation"

Explain the importance of molasses (sugar) to the northern colonies' thriving rum industry. Point out that tax stamps were applied to such things as playing cards, newspapers, and legal documents. Make sure the students understand the meaning of the phrase, "No Taxation Without Representation."

3-C. The Townshend Acts

Explain that Charles Townshend was Chancellor of the Exchequer, or head of the department in charge of British government revenue. Challenge the students to identify someone in a similar government position in the United States today. Ask them what would motivate someone in this type of position. Make sure the students know that the boycott of British goods led to the repeal of the Townshend Acts, except for the law about taxes on tea.

3-D. The Boston Massacre

Point out that the five American victims of this event were the first people to die protesting against the British. One American victim was Crispus Attucks, who was a man of African descent. Make sure the students understand that the American crowd was taunting the British soldiers. Then, ask the students if they think the term "massacre" is justified.

3-E. The Boston Tea Party

The Boston Tea Party was a direct protest against the Tea Act, passed in 1773. After the Townshend Acts were passed placing taxes on tea, the colonists refused to purchase tea from the British and began buying from other sources. Since the British East India Company was losing money, the Tea Act was passed to allow the company to sell tea to the colonists at lower costs.

3-F. The Intolerable Acts

The Intolerable Acts were a direct result of the Boston Tea Party. They were designed to punish the people who were involved and to reassert British authority. Challenge the students to explain what they would have done after the Boston Tea Party if they were part of the British government.

3-G. The First Continental Congress

Make sure the students understand that the goal of this meeting was not independence but greater rights for the American colonies. The Continental Congress met in secret at Carpenters' Hall, since it was among the largest buildings in Philadelphia at the time.

3-H. The War Begins

Share with the students Ralph Waldo Emerson's hymn in memorial to Concord:

> "By the rude bridge that arched the flood
>
> Their flag to April's breeze unfurled
>
> Here once the embattled farmers stood
>
> And fired the shot heard 'round the world.'"

Discuss the meaning of each line with the students. Emphasize the words, "the shot heard 'round the world," in the last line.

3-I. A Voice From the Past: The Declaration of Independence

If appropriate, allude to the roots of this passage in Enlightenment thought, especially that of John Locke.

3-J. Map Study: Battles of the Revolutionary War

Have the students consult the appropriate maps in their textbooks and in encyclopedia articles.

3-K. Biography: George Washington

Point out that George Washington valued his character and his reputation above all else and that he worked diligently throughout his life to be a man of good character.

3-L. The Treaty of Paris

Make sure the students include the fishing provision, which gave American fishermen rights to fish the Grand Banks. Explain how important the fishing industry was to the young American economy.

3-M. Map Study: The United States in 1783

Point out that the United States was primarily rural and that, even though the territory of the new country stretched far to the west, the population of the United States was primarily concentrated on or near the east coast. Have the students compare the American population in 1783 to the population of a major city today.

3-N. The Time Machine: Food

Help the students identify the main points of the essay, which should be written in the left-hand circle of the Venn diagram.

3-O. A Postcard From the Past: Independence National Historical Park

Suggest that the students visit www.nps.gov (the web site of the National Park Service) to gather information about Independence National Historical Park.

The Revolutionary Period

In the box below, draw a picture or attach a picture from a magazine or the Internet that represents this period of American history. The picture can be of anything you think is appropriate.

Ask questions about this period of American history. Then, answer them.

Question: WHO_____?

Answer:_____

Question: WHAT_____?

Answer:_____

Question: WHERE _____?

Answer:_____

Question: WHEN _____?

Answer:_____

Question: WHY _____?

Answer:_____

Question: HOW_____?

Answer:_____

This important date in American history is brought to you by

_____

"No Taxation Without Representation"

Complete the diagram below.

CAUSES

EFFECTS

THE SUGAR ACT

THE STAMP ACT

Explain the meaning of the phrase, "No taxation without representation."

_____

_____

This important date in American history is brought to you by

_____

Complete the diagram below.

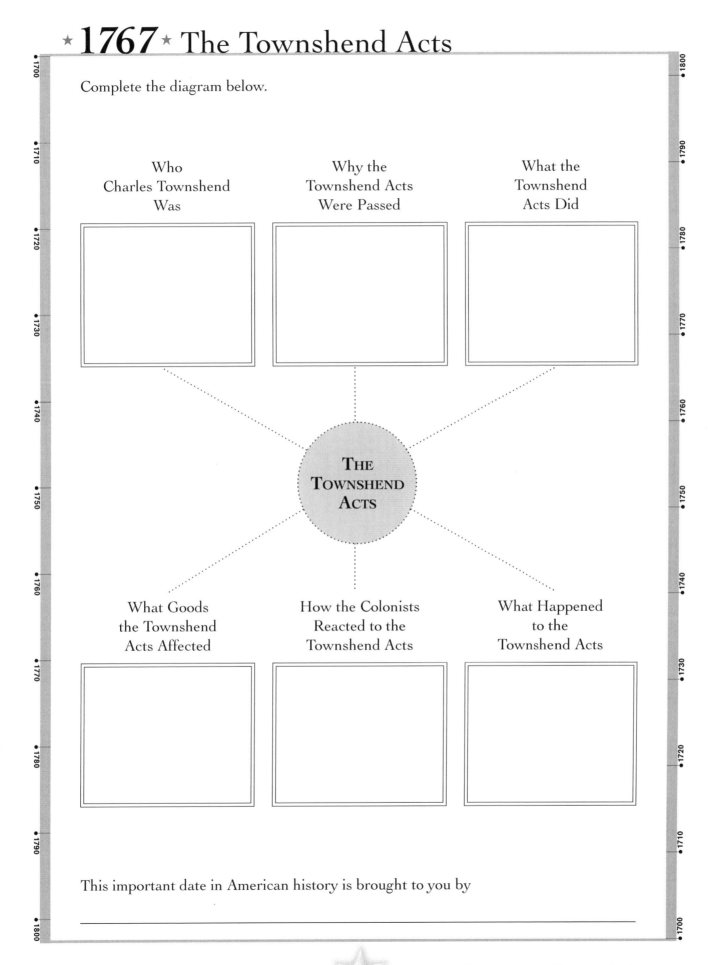

Who
Charles Townshend
Was

Why the
Townshend Acts
Were Passed

What the
Townshend
Acts Did

THE
TOWNSHEND
ACTS

What Goods
the Townshend
Acts Affected

How the Colonists
Reacted to the
Townshend Acts

What Happened
to the
Townshend Acts

This important date in American history is brought to you by

Study the illustration below. Then, complete the writing activities.

Imagine that you are one of the colonists. Write a sentence that describes this scene. Then, explain why you think your actions are justified.

_____

_____

_____

_____

Imagine that you are one of the soldiers. Write a sentence that describes this scene. Then, explain why you think your actions are justified.

_____

_____

_____

This important date in American history is brought to you by

_____

Study the illustration below. Then, write a caption for it that tells about the Boston Tea Party. Your caption should tell what the Boston Tea Party was, who was involved, and why these people did what they did.

_____

_____

_____

_____

_____

This important date in American history is brought to you by

_____

Complete the chart below. Then, complete the sentence.

THE INTOLERABLE ACTS

Name of Act	Purpose of Act	What It Required	Main Effect of Acts

The colonists called these the "Intolerable Acts" because _____

_____

_____

This important date in American history is brought to you by

_____

★1774★ The First Continental Congress

The First Continental Congress met at Carpenters' Hall in Philadelphia. What might you have overheard if you were there? Complete the diagram below to answer this question.

"We are meeting because…

"We want to tell King George III that…

"Some of our leaders are…

"We have set up the Continental Association to…

"We will meet again if…

This important date in American history is brought to you by

Explain what happened at each place.

American Soldier
("Minuteman")

Lexington

_____

_____

_____

_____

_____

Concord

_____

_____

_____

_____

_____

British Soldier
("Redcoat")

This important date in American history is brought to you by

_____

The Declaration of Independence

On July 4, 1776, the Second Continental Congress approved the Declaration of Independence. Read the section from the Declaration of Independence below. Then, answer the questions.

> *"We hold these truths to be self-evident [obvious], that all men are created equal, that they are endowed by their Creator with certain unalienable [undeniable] Rights, that among these are Life, Liberty and the pursuit of Happiness. That, to secure these rights, Governments are instituted [set up] among Men, deriving their just powers from the consent of the governed."*

What "truths" does the Declaration of Independence say are "self-evident," or obvious?

_____

_____

_____

_____

According to the Declaration of Independence, what is the purpose of government?

_____

_____

_____

_____

This important date in American history is brought to you by

_____

Battles of the Revolutionary War

Label the following items on the map below: the 13 colonies, several major cities, major bodies of water, and the major battles of the Revolutionary War (including dates). Make a key for your map. Your key should include symbols for cities and battles.

MAP KEY

This important date in American history is brought to you by

★ George Washington ★

Answer the questions below.

GEORGE WASHINGTON

When did he live? _____

Why is George Washington called the "Father

of Our Country"? _____

_____

What role did he play in the Revolutionary War?

_____

_____

_____

_____

_____

What was his home called? _____

One of Washington's officers wrote the following about Washington: "First in war, first in peace, and first in the hearts of his countrymen." Explain what this means.

_____

_____

_____

_____

_____

This important date in American history is brought to you by

_____

The Treaty of Paris officially ended the war between the Americans and the British. List the major provisions, or requirements, of the Treaty of Paris.

The Treaty of Paris

1. _____

_____

2. _____

_____

3. _____

_____

4. _____

_____

5. _____

_____

This important date in American history is brought to you by

_____

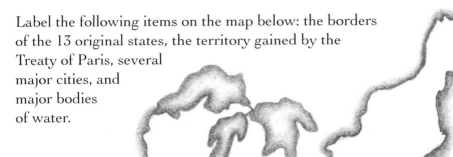

Label the following items on the map below: the borders of the 13 original states, the territory gained by the Treaty of Paris, several major cities, and major bodies of water.

In 1783, there were about 3.1 million Americans. They lived in rural (country) and urban (city) areas. Use the information below to create a circle graph.

Percentage of Americans
Living in Rural Areas: 96%

Percentage of Americans
Living in Urban Areas: 4%

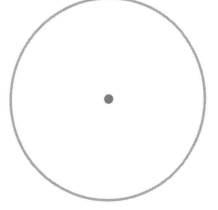

This important date in American history is brought to you by

_____

Activate the Time Machine to learn about food in North America during the colonial period. In the left-hand circle, write facts about food during that time. In the right-hand circle, write facts about food today. In the space where the circles overlap, write facts about food that both time periods have in common.

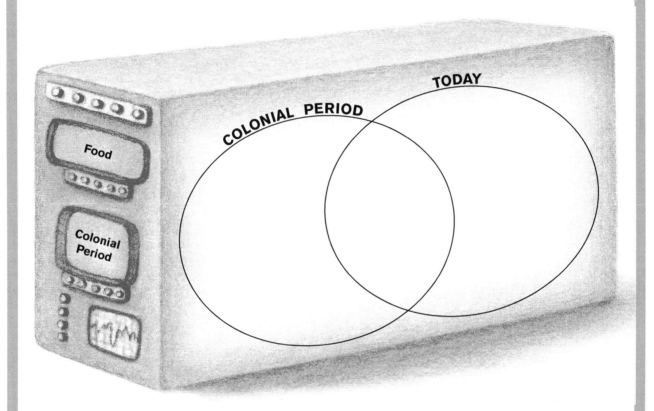

Most families in the new United States of America lived on farms. They provided almost all of their food for themselves.

Meat was an important part of their diet. There were many kinds of meat. Farmers raised cattle, hogs, sheep, and chicken. People also hunted for other types of meat, like deer, squirrel, and turkey and caught many types of fish from streams and the ocean.

Bread was also important. The most common kind of bread was cornbread, which was either baked or fried. In addition, the colonists made wheat and rye breads.

A typical breakfast in colonial times might have been meat and bread. A typical dinner might have been meat and vegetable stew. Whatever the meal was, it was usually accompanied by a beverage. The colonists drank tea, hot chocolate, beer, wine, and rum.

This important trip into American history is brought to you by

_____

Independence Hall, in Philadelphia, Pennsylvania, is where the Second Continental Congress met. This was the place the Declaration of Independence was issued from. Today, Independence Hall is part of Independence National Historical Park. What would it be like to visit this park? Conduct research to find out.

Use the Internet or any other resources your teacher suggests. Read the articles, and study the illustrations. When you have gathered enough information, make a postcard.

On the front of the postcard, draw a picture or attach a picture from a magazine or the Internet that gives some information about Independence Hall. On the back of the postcard, write a caption that explains the picture. Then, write a note to a friend that tells why Independence Hall is an important part of American history.

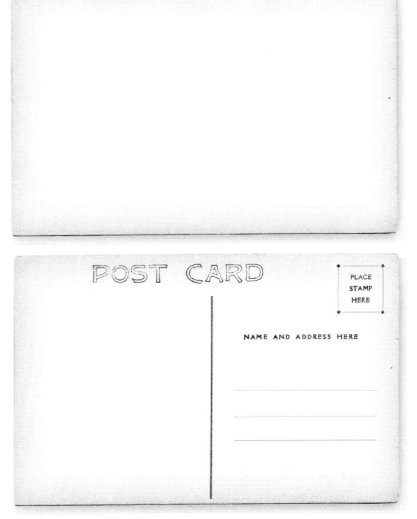

POST CARD

PLACE STAMP HERE

NAME AND ADDRESS HERE

This important period in American history is brought to you by

UNIT 4 — Creating the Constitution ★ TEACHING NOTES ★

1781–1803

UNIT OVERVIEW

The Constitution, written at the Constitutional Convention in 1787 and ratified the following year, is one of the most important documents in American history. This unit is devoted to the Constitution's inception, ratification, modification, and interpretation during the first years after the United States was established.

Activity Sheet 4-A provides a unit overview. Activity Sheet 4-B focuses on the Articles of Confederation, the nation's first plan of government. The Articles of Confederation failed to establish a strong central government. This resulted in such crises as Shays' Rebellion, covered on Activity Sheet 4-C. The Constitutional Convention was called to create a new plan of government for the young United States. Activity Sheet 4-D focuses on the Constitutional Convention. Activity Sheet 4-E is a biographical study of two of the Constitutional Convention's more prominent delegates, Benjamin Franklin and James Madison, the "Father of the Constitution." After the Constitution was written, it had to be ratified. The bitter debate over ratification between the Federalists and the Anti-Federalists is the focus of Activity Sheet 4-F.

Activity Sheets 4-G through 4-L address the Constitution, including the Preamble; the structure of the Articles; the guarantees provided by the Bill of Rights; and the principles of federalism, separation of powers, and checks and balances.

Activity Sheet 4-M introduces the students to Marbury v. Madison, the court case that established the Supreme Court's right to decide whether legislative and executive actions are constitutional (judicial review).

The Time Machine Activity, Activity Sheet 4-N, compares housing today to housing during the late 1700s. A Postcard From the Past, Activity Sheet 4-O, is about the National Archives in Washington, D.C., where the original Constitution is displayed.

FOCUS ACTIVITIES

To focus the students' attention on this period of American history, consider the following activities:

It's Your Right

Ask the students what rights they have. List their responses on the board. Then, challenge the students to categorize specific rights under more general headings (for example, their right to attend an art club meeting is in the "Freedom of Assembly" category). Segue into a discussion about the Bill of Rights.

Visiting Washington…

Invite the students who have visited Washington, D.C., to describe some of the national landmarks they saw on their trips. If none of the students have been to Washington, D.C., ask them what they would like to see if they did visit. After a brief discussion of the more prominent locations (for example, the Washington Monument), discuss the National Archives. Explain that one of the most precious items in its collection is the Constitution.

Because It's Unconstitutional

Ask the students whether some obviously unconstitutional laws (for example, a ban on public meetings) could ever pass in the United States. Have the students think of other laws that could not be passed because they would be unconstitutional. Ask the students why such laws are forbidden. Explain that the Constitution is the highest authority in the United States.

CONSTRUCTING THE TIMELINE

This unit consists of 15 activity sheets that focus on significant events, people, and places related to the period during which the Constitution was created and ratified. Each activity sheet is designed to, once completed, become part of a posted classroom timeline of the period covered in the unit.

The Introduction (pages VII–XVI) provides a detailed explanation of how to use the activity sheets in the classroom and suggests various ways to construct the timeline using the completed activity sheets.

You can construct the timeline any way you see fit. Use the Timeline Components (pages XVIII–XXVI) to connect the activity sheets. Below are two possible timelines, constructed from the activity sheets in this unit and the Timeline Components.

Option 1: Basic Timeline

Construct this timeline to identify only the essential elements of the period.

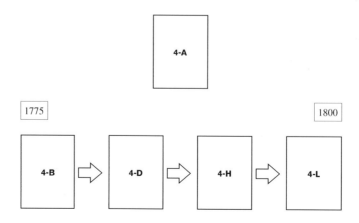

Option 2: Complete Timeline

Construct this timeline to identify the essential elements of the period, examine them in greater detail, and extend student learning.

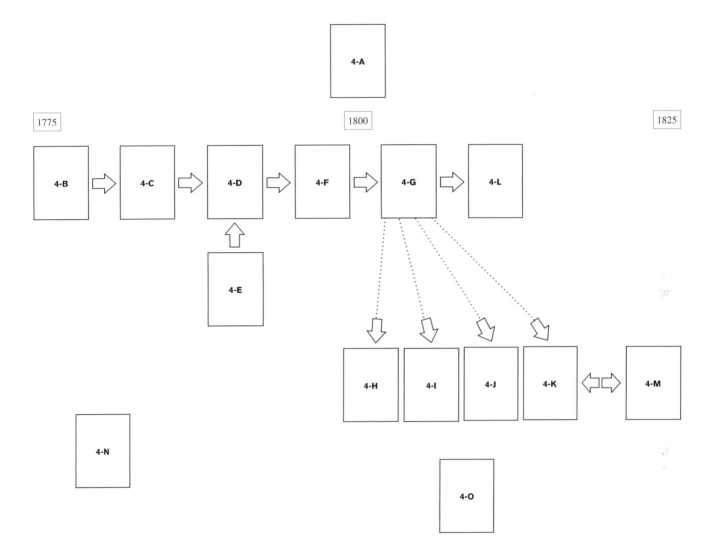

CRITICAL THINKING SKILLS

The activity sheets in this unit address various critical thinking skills. In addition, the constructed timeline emphasizes the essential critical thinking skills of identifying main ideas and details, sequencing events, and relating causes and effects.

Identifying Main Ideas and Details

Point out that Activity Sheet 4-A outlines the main ideas of the unit. Explain that the topics of the other activity sheets in the unit reflect the main ideas of the historical period the students are studying. Further explain that some activity sheets focus on the details related to specific topics.

As you and the students construct the timeline, show them that the following activity sheets form a main idea/detail relationship: 4-D/4-E, 4-G/4-H, 4-I, 4-J, and 4-K. Have the students annotate the Timeline Arrows appropriately. Challenge the students to find similar relationships or create them by rearranging the activity sheets.

Sequencing Events

Point out that the activity sheets that make up the timeline are sequential. Show the students how the Timeline Dates provide a concrete reference for when events happened and how they relate to other events. (For example, the Constitution was written in 1787 before the Bill of Rights was written in 1791.) Make sure the students see that the Timeline Arrows indicate a chronological flow from left to right.

Relating Causes and Effects

As you and the students construct the timeline, show them that Activity Sheets 4-B, 4-C, 4-D, 4-F, 4-G, and 4-L form a cause-and-effect chain. Point out that the principle of checks and balances addressed by the Constitution, covered on Activity Sheet 4-K, is a cause of the court case discussed on Activity Sheet 4-M. Have the students annotate the Timeline Arrows appropriately. Challenge the students to find similar relationships or create them by rearranging the activity sheets.

INDIVIDUAL ACTIVITY SHEET NOTES

The notes below provide a variety of tips on how to guide the students through the completion and extension of each activity sheet.

4-A. Creating the Constitution

This activity is most appropriate for the students to complete with partners, in small groups, or as a whole class. For example, you might want to complete the questions with the whole class at the beginning of the unit and then have the students answer the questions at the end of the unit. Encourage the students to think of additional questions related to the topic.

4-B. The Articles of Confederation

Emphasize that the Articles of Confederation failed to establish a strong central government. Explain that this was a natural result of the Americans' experience under British monarchial rule.

4-C. Shays' Rebellion

Explain that Shays' Rebellion was a result of the failures of the Articles of Confederation. Point out that Shays' Rebellion was a major reason for the calling of the Constitutional Convention.

4-D. The Constitutional Convention

You might want to have the students create a mock government for their classroom. Ask the students the following questions about the new student government: How will it be organized? Who will have power? How will the leaders be chosen? Point out that these questions are very challenging and that they also had to be answered at the Constitutional Convention.

4-E. Biography: James Madison and Benjamin Franklin

Focus the students' attention on the commanding role James Madison played at the Constitutional Convention (and later, during the ratification debate, as one of the authors of *The Federalist*). Discuss the wide-ranging accomplishments of Benjamin Franklin as an inventor, an author, and a statesman.

4-F. The Federalists and the Anti-Federalists

Help the students see the connection between the arguments of the Anti-Federalists and the prevailing anti-government spirit of the American Revolution.

4-G. The Constitution

Have the students read some of the Constitution. Remind them that it is the highest authority in the United States. This means that local, state, and federal government actions must not violate the Constitution. Point out that this document has stood the test of time and that it is widely envied and copied all over the world.

4-H. A Voice From the Past: The Preamble to the Constitution

You might want to have the students memorize the Preamble. Challenge them to identify current government actions that implement the goals listed in the Preamble.

4-I. Federalism

Tell the students that another name for federalism is the federal system. Ask them to identify the advantages and disadvantages of this system. Point out that the delegated, concurrent, and reserved powers are identified in the Constitution.

4-J. Separation of Powers

Have the students memorize the names and the basic functions of the three branches of government. Ask the students to name the officials and groups that compose each branch. Discuss why the Founders thought it was a good idea to separate the powers of government among three branches.

4-K. Checks and Balances

Tell the students that in the arrows they should write an explanation of how the branches of government check each other. Challenge the students to explain why this system is called "checks and balances."

4-L. The Bill of Rights

Remind the students that the inclusion of the Bill of Rights was a concession to the Anti-Federalists. Ask the students if they think any other rights should have been included.

4-M. *Marbury* v. *Madison*

Make sure the students understand the concept of judicial review and that it was established because of this landmark Supreme Court case. Explain that before *Marbury* v. *Madison*, the role of the Supreme Court was unclear. Since then, exercising judicial review has become its primary function.

4-N. The Time Machine: Housing

Help the students identify the main points of the essay, which should be written in the left-hand circle of the Venn diagram. Ask interested students to conduct research to find photographs of housing during the late 1700s. Allow the students to present their photographs to the class.

4-O. A Postcard From the Past: The National Archives

Suggest that the students visit www.archives.gov to gather information about the National Archives.

Creating the Constitution

In the box below, draw a picture or attach a picture from a magazine or the Internet that represents this period of American history. The picture can be of anything you think is appropriate.

Ask questions about this period of American history. Then, answer them.

Question: WHO_____?

Answer:_____

Question: WHAT_____?

Answer:_____

Question: WHERE_____?

Answer:_____

Question: WHEN_____?

Answer:_____

Question: WHY_____?

Answer:_____

Question: HOW_____?

Answer:_____

This important date in American history is brought to you by

_____

★ 1781 ★ The Articles of Confederation

Complete the chart below.

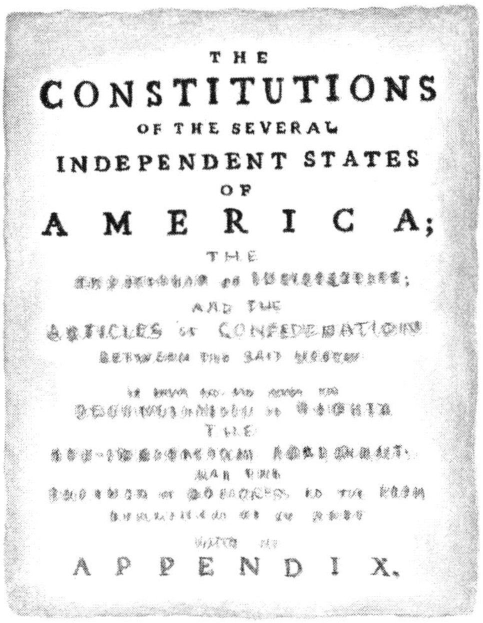

THE
CONSTITUTIONS
OF THE SEVERAL
INDEPENDENT STATES
OF
AMERICA;
THE
AND THE
APPENDIX.

THE ARTICLES OF CONFEDERATION

Who Created It	
Why It Was Created	
Its Main Weaknesses	

This important date in American history is brought to you by

____

Complete the diagram below.

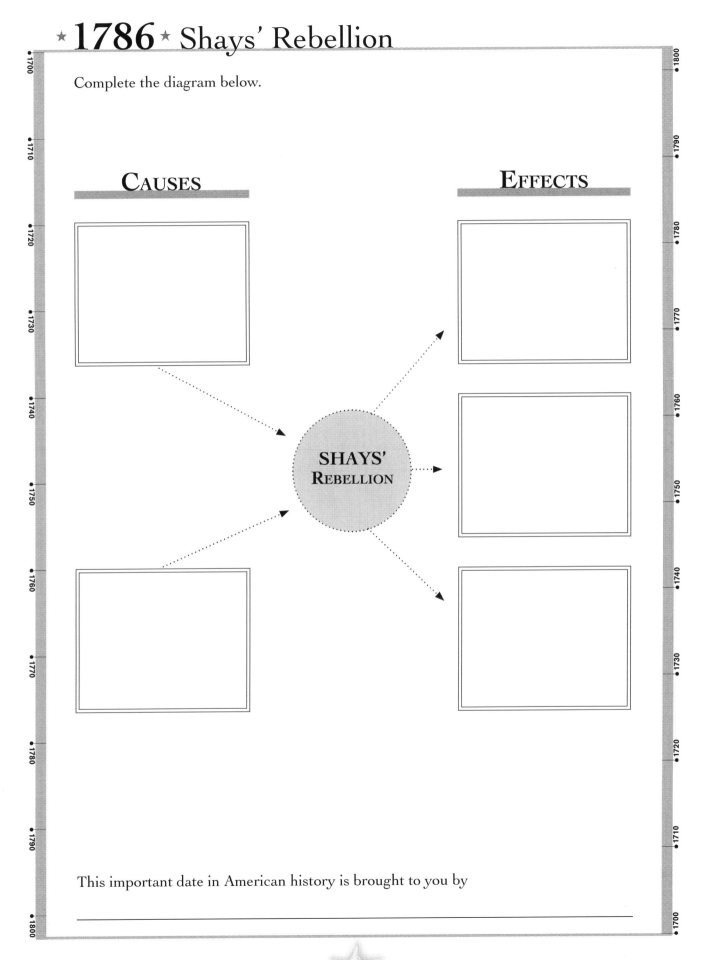

CAUSES

EFFECTS

SHAYS'
REBELLION

This important date in American history is brought to you by

72

Study the illustration below. Then, write a caption for it that tells about the Constitutional Convention. Your caption should tell what the Constitutional Convention was, where it was held, and what its result was.

_____

_____

_____

_____

_____

This important date in American history is brought to you by

_____

★1787★ James Madison and Benjamin Franklin

Answer the questions below.

JAMES MADISON

When did he live? _____

What were his major accomplishments? _____

_____

_____

Why is James Madison called the "Father of the Constitution"?

_____

_____

BENJAMIN FRANKLIN

When did he live? _____

What were his major accomplishments? _____

_____

_____

When asked if the Constitutional Convention created a monarchy or a republic, Franklin responded by saying, "A republic, if you can keep it." What did he mean?

_____

_____

_____

This important date in American history is brought to you by

_____

The Federalists and the Anti-Federalists

Complete the diagram below.

THE FEDERALISTS

Their Arguments for the Constitution

_____

_____

_____

_____

_____

_____

What was _The Federalist_?

_____

_____

_____

_____

_____

John Jay

James Madison

Alexander Hamilton

THE ANTI-FEDERALISTS

Their Arguments Against the Constitution

_____

_____

_____

_____

_____

_____

_____

_____

_____

Thomas Paine

Patrick Henry

George Mason

We the People

Article 1

This important date in American history is brought to you by

_____

1700 1710 1720 1730 1740 1750 1760 1770 1780 1790 1800

1800 1790 1780 1770 1760 1750 1740 1730 1720 1710 1700

Complete the chart below.

Articles of the Constitution

Section	Subject/Purpose
Article I	
Article II	
Article III	
Article IV	
Article V	
Article VI	
Article VII	

This important date in American history is brought to you by

_____

Read the Preamble to the Constitution. Then, answer the questions.

"We the People of the United States, in order to form a more perfect Union, establish justice, insure domestic tranquility, provide for the common defense, promote the general welfare, and secure the blessings of liberty to ourselves and our posterity [future generations], do ordain and establish this Constitution for the United States of America."

Why is it important that the Preamble begins with the words, "We the People"?

_____

_____

What are the reasons the Preamble lists for creating the Constitution?

_____

_____

What is meant by the term "general welfare"?

_____

_____

This important date in American history is brought to you by

_____

★ 1787 ★ Federalism

Complete the diagram below. Then, write a definition for the term "Federalism."

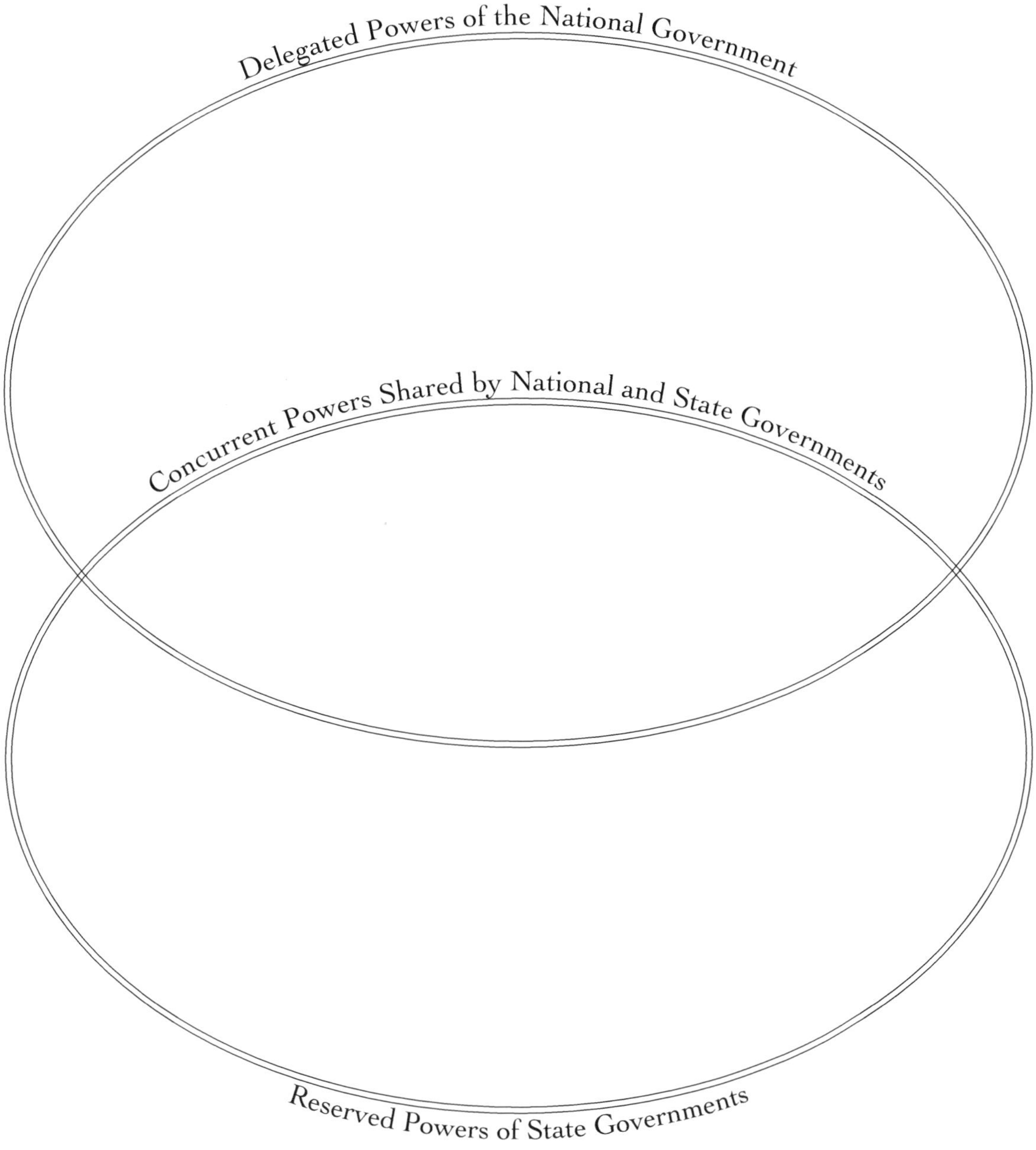

Delegated Powers of the National Government

Concurrent Powers Shared by National and State Governments

Reserved Powers of State Governments

Federalism: _____

_____

This important date in American history is brought to you by

_____

★ 1700
● 1710
● 1720
● 1730
● 1740
● 1750
● 1760
● 1770
● 1780
● 1790
● 1800

● 1800
● 1790
● 1780
● 1770
● 1760
● 1750
● 1740
● 1730
● 1720
● 1710
● 1700

★1787★ Separation of Powers

Complete the diagram below. In each circle, draw a symbol that represents one of the three branches of government. Identify and explain the purpose of each branch. Then, write a definition for the term "separation of powers."

Branch of Government:

Purpose:

Branch of Government:

Purpose:

Branch of Government:

Purpose:

Separation of Powers: _____

_____

This important date in American history is brought to you by

_____

★ 1787 ★ Checks and Balances

Complete the diagram below by writing the check or balance on the arrow line. Then, write a definition for the term "checks and balances."

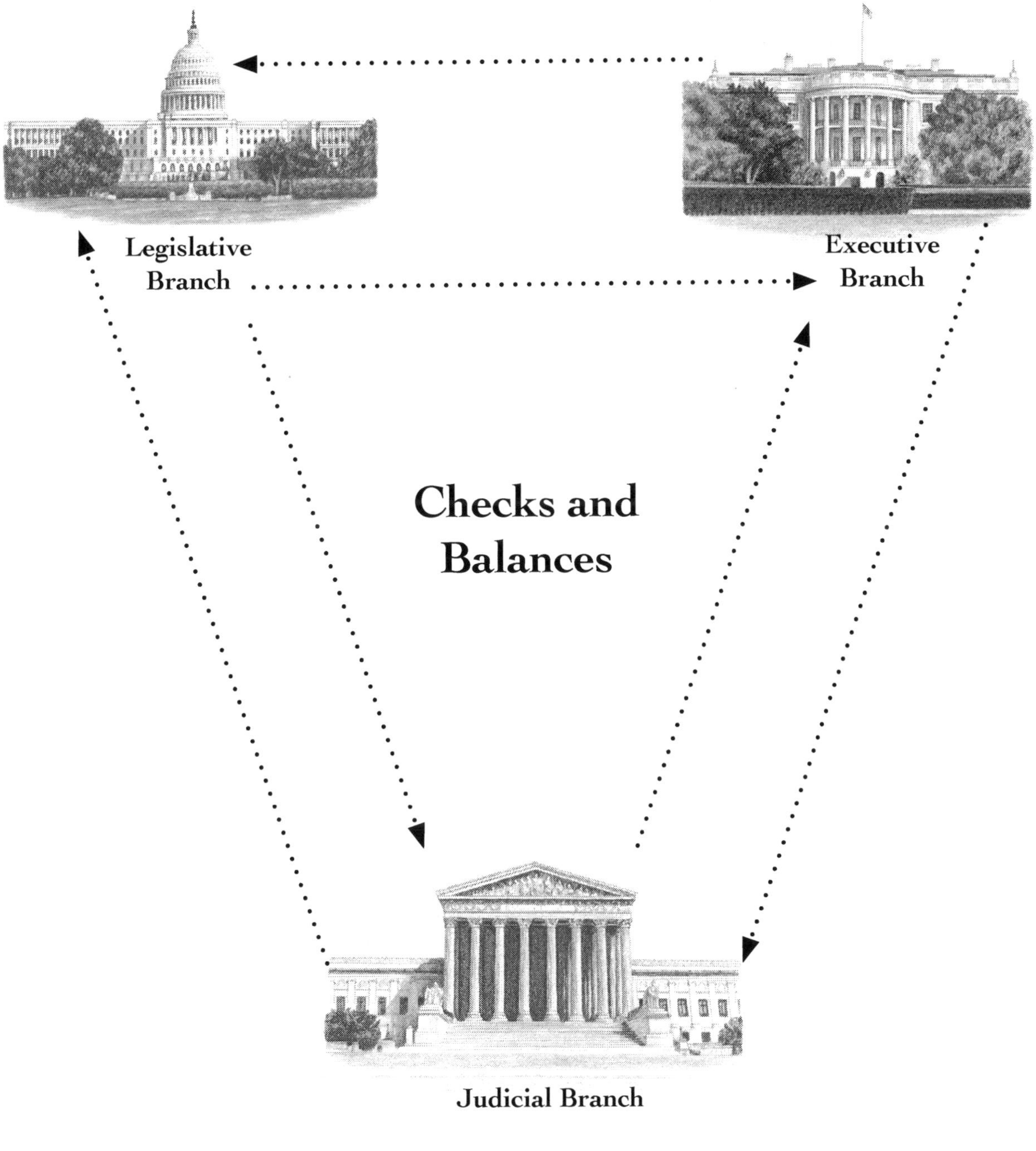

Legislative Branch
Executive Branch
Checks and Balances
Judicial Branch

Checks and Balances: ____

____

This important date in American history is brought to you by

____

Complete the chart below.

The Bill of Rights

Amendment	Freedom or Rights Guaranteed
First	
Second	
Third	
Fourth	
Fifth	
Sixth	
Seventh	
Eighth	
Ninth	
Tenth	

This important date in American history is brought to you by

_____

Explain what *Marbury* v. *Madison* was about and the result of the case. Then, write a definition for the term "judicial review."

The Case: _____

_____

_____

The Result: _____

_____

_____

Judicial Review: _____

_____

_____

This important date in American history is brought to you by

_____

Activate the Time Machine to learn about housing during the late 1700s. In the left-hand circle, write facts about housing during that time. In the right-hand circle, write facts about housing today. In the space where the circles overlap, write facts about housing that both time periods have in common.

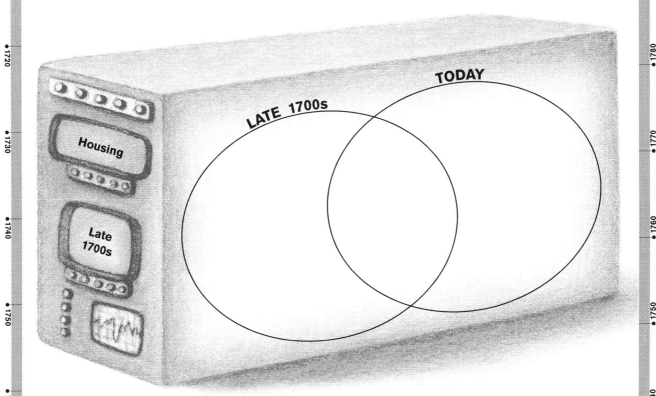

Most Americans in the country's early years lived on farms. So, most people lived in farmhouses. These houses were usually made of wood. This should come as no surprise since one of the things that attracted settlers to America was the land's vast forests.

There was a wide variety of farmhouse styles in early America. This is because immigrants from different countries built houses that were similar to the ones built in their homelands.

Many people usually lived in each farmhouse, including children and their parents, grandparents, aunts, uncles, and cousins. Servants and slaves often lived nearby.

This important trip into American history is brought to you by

_____

The National Archives and Records Administration is part of the federal government. It is in charge of maintaining valuable records. Exhibition Hall at the National Archives Building in Washington, D.C., is where many historic records are displayed for the public. What is it like to visit Exhibition Hall? Conduct research to find out.

Use the Internet or any other resources your teacher suggests. Read the articles, and study the illustrations. When you have gathered enough information, make a postcard.

On the front of the postcard, draw a picture or attach a picture from a magazine or the Internet that gives some information about Exhibition Hall. On the back of the postcard, write a caption that explains the picture. Then, write a note to a friend about things to do and see at Exhibition Hall.

POST CARD

PLACE STAMP HERE

NAME AND ADDRESS HERE

This important place in American history is brought to you by

_____

UNIT 5 Expanding the Country   ★ TEACHING NOTES ★

1790–1860

UNIT OVERVIEW

The growth of the United States from a relatively small strip of land on the east coast to a country stretching "from sea to shining sea" is one of the most important and dramatic developments of modern times. The expansion happened quickly; by 1853, all of the territory that would become the contiguous 48 states was controlled by the United States. This unit focuses on this territorial growth. Units 6 and 7 address other historical developments during the first half of the nineteenth century.

Activity Sheet 5-A provides a unit overview. Activity Sheet 5-B sets a baseline at the year 1790, when the first census was held. Activity Sheets 5-C through 5-E focus on the Louisiana Purchase and its exploration. Activity Sheet 5-F addresses the lesser-known, but still important, Red River and Florida Cessions.

Activity Sheet 5-G explores the concept of Manifest Destiny, which took hold in the minds of Americans during the 1830s. Both a cause and an outgrowth of Manifest Destiny, the Oregon Trail is the subject of Activity Sheet 5-H. Activity Sheets 5-I through 5-K address three more major territorial acquisitions: the Texas Annexation, the Oregon Country Cession, and the Mexican Cession. Together, these acquisitions finally brought the western border of the United States to the Pacific Ocean.

Activity Sheets 5-L and 5-M are about the California Gold Rush. Activity Sheet 5-N addresses the Santa Fe Trail. Activity Sheet 5-O focuses on the Gadsden Purchase, which, in 1853, completed the country's acquisition of the territory that would become the Lower 48 States. Activity Sheet 5-P illustrates the net result of territorial growth in an 1860 map of the country and provides a dramatic contrast with the map of the country in 1790 that opened the unit.

The Time Machine Activity, Activity Sheet 5-Q, compares entertainment today to entertainment during the first half of the 1800s. A Postcard From the Past, Activity Sheet 5-R, is about the Santa Fe National Historic Trail.

FOCUS ACTIVITIES

To focus the students' attention on this period of American history, consider the following activities:

Sacagawea

Show the students a Sacagawea dollar coin, and pass it around the classroom. Ask the students to share what they know about this remarkable woman and why she is honored on the coin. Expand the discussion to include the Lewis and Clark Expedition and the Louisiana Purchase.

Who Lived Here?

Ask the students who the original inhabitants of their community were. Then, ask the students who lived in their community next. Draw a flowchart on the board that shows the different groups of people who have lived in the community over time. Challenge the students to explain how their community became part of the United States.

Trails West

Invite the students to describe the longest journeys they have ever taken on foot. Point out that many of the people who headed west walked most of the way; many of them walked as far as 2,000 miles! Ask the students what they picture when they think about the early settlers migrating westward along the Oregon and Santa Fe Trails.

CONSTRUCTING THE TIMELINE

This unit consists of 18 activity sheets that focus on significant events, people, and places related to the westward expansion of the United States. Each activity sheet is designed to, once completed, become part of a posted classroom timeline of the period covered in the unit.

The Introduction (pages VII–XVI) provides a detailed explanation of how to use the activity sheets in the classroom and suggests various ways to construct the timeline using the completed activity sheets.

You can construct the timeline any way you see fit. Use the Timeline Components (pages XVIII–XXVI) to connect the activity sheets. Below are two possible timelines, constructed from the activity sheets in this unit and the Timeline Components.

Option 1: Basic Timeline

Construct this timeline to identify only the essential elements of the period.

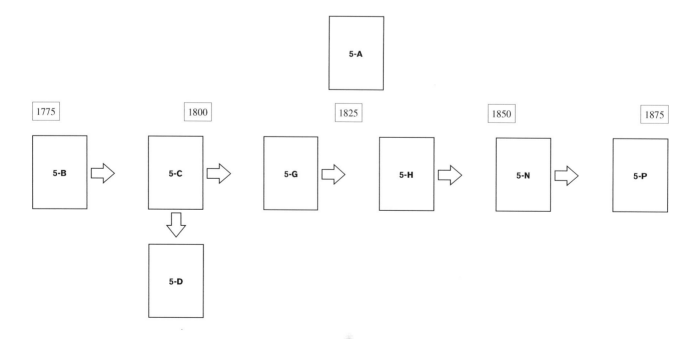

Option 2: Complete Timeline

Construct this timeline to identify the essential elements of the period, examine them in greater detail, and extend student learning.

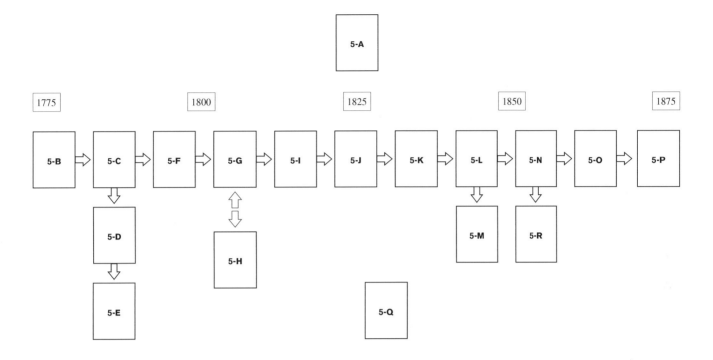

CRITICAL THINKING SKILLS

The activity sheets in this unit address various critical thinking skills. In addition, the constructed timeline emphasizes the essential critical thinking skills of identifying main ideas and details, sequencing events, and relating causes and effects.

Identifying Main Ideas and Details

Point out that Activity Sheet 5-A outlines the main ideas of the unit. Explain that the topics of the other activity sheets in the unit reflect the main ideas of the historical period the students are studying. Further explain that some activity sheets focus on the details related to specific topics.

As you and the students construct the timeline, show them that the following activity sheets form main idea/detail relationships: 5-C/5-D, 5-D/5-E, 5-G/5-H, 5-L/5-M, and 5-N/5-R. Have the students annotate the Timeline Arrows appropriately. Challenge the students to find similar relationships or create them by rearranging the activity sheets.

Sequencing Events

Point out that the activity sheets that make up the timeline are sequential. Show the students how the Timeline Dates provide a concrete reference for when events happened and how they relate to other events. (For example, the Louisiana Purchase was in 1803 before the Lewis and Clark Expedition in 1804 through 1806.) Make sure the students see that the Timeline Arrows indicate a chronological flow from left to right.

The emphasis of this unit is on sequence, specifically the sequence of territorial acquisitions of the United States during the first half of the nineteenth century.

Relating Causes and Effects

As you and the students construct the timeline, show them that the following activity sheets form cause/effect relationships: 5-C/5-D, 5-D/5-E, and 5-G/5-H. Have the students annotate the Timeline Arrows appropriately. Challenge the students to find similar relationships or create them by rearranging the activity sheets.

INDIVIDUAL ACTIVITY SHEET NOTES

The notes below provide a variety of tips on how to guide the students through the completion and extension of each activity sheet.

5-A. Expanding the Country

This activity is most appropriate for the students to complete with partners, in small groups, or as a whole class. For example, you might want to complete the questions with the whole class at the beginning of the unit and then have the students answer sthe questions at the end of the unit. Encourage the students to think of additional questions related to the topic.

5-B. Map Study: The United States in 1790

Make sure the students understand what the census is and that it is conducted every ten years. Explain that 1790 was the year of the first United States census.

5-C. The Louisiana Purchase

Emphasize the incredible size of the area purchased and its relatively low price. Ask the students why they think France would be willing to part with such valuable territory.

5-D. The Lewis and Clark Expedition

This expedition is one of the most fabled in American history. It is also the subject of many books and films. Encourage the students to do outside reading about this highly interesting voyage, or consider showing a film about it in class.

5-E. Biography: Sacagawea

Use the students' study of Sacagawea to emphasize the vital role Native Americans played in helping European and American explorers and settlers for centuries.

5-F. The Florida Cession

Have one of the students consult a dictionary and define the word "cession" for the class, explaining what the word means in this context.

5-G. Manifest Destiny

Make sure the students understand the concept of Manifest Destiny, and challenge them to think of similar widespread beliefs held in the United States today. Ask the students whether they think the belief of Manifest Destiny was justified. Allow them to debate their opinions.

5-H. The Oregon Trail

Emphasize how difficult and tiring it was to travel along the Oregon Trail. Tell the students that many people died. Have the students trace the route of the Oregon Trail on a modern highway map of the United States so that they understand how far the settlers traveled.

5-I. The Texas Annexation

Accompany the assignment of this activity sheet with a mini-lecture on the history of Texas and the Texas Revolution, the Republic of Texas, and its annexation as a state.

5-J. The Oregon Country Cession

Point out that this acquisition brought the border of the United States to the Pacific Ocean for the first time and established the forty-ninth parallel as the northern boundary of the country in this region.

5-K. The Mexican Cession

Make sure the students understand that the Mexican Cession was a result of the Mexican War, which lasted from 1846 to 1848.

5-L. The California Gold Rush

Share some of the lore about this remarkable event, including the birth of Levi jeans and the term "Forty-Niner."

5-M. A Voice From the Past: San Francisco During the Gold Rush

Explain that this description of San Francisco during its boomtown days might very well have applied to numerous boomtowns across the western United States during the period of American expansion.

5-N. The Santa Fe Trail

Have the students compare and contrast the nature and purpose of the Santa Fe Trail and the nature and purpose of the Oregon Trail.

5-O. The Gadsden Purchase

Make sure the students understand that this purchase was made partly to clarify the boundary between the United States and Mexico (left unclear by the Treaty of Guadalupe Hidalgo, which ended the Mexican War) and largely to provide a southern railroad route to the West Coast.

5-P. Map Study: The United States in 1860

Have the students compare and contrast this map and the map of the United States in 1790 on Activity Sheet 5-B to emphasize the phenomenal growth of the United States during the first half of the nineteenth century.

5-Q. The Time Machine: Entertainment

Help the students identify the main points of the essay, which should be written in the left-hand circle of the Venn diagram.

5-R. A Postcard From the Past: The Santa Fe National Historic Trail

Suggest that the students visit www.nps.gov (the web site of the National Park Service) to gather information about the Santa Fe National Historic Trail.

Expanding the Country

In the box below, draw a picture or attach a picture from a magazine or the Internet that represents this period of American history. The picture can be of anything you think is appropriate.

Ask questions about this period of American history. Then, answer them.

Question: WHO_____?

Answer:_____

Question: WHAT_____?

Answer:_____

Question: WHERE _____?

Answer:_____

Question: WHEN _____?

Answer:_____

Question: WHY_____?

Answer:_____

Question: HOW_____?

Answer:_____

This important date in American history is brought to you by

_____

Label the following items on the map below:

- state borders in 1790,
- territories held by the United States in 1790,
- territories held by other countries in 1790,
- several major cities, and
- major bodies of water.

The first census was taken in 1790. Research its findings, and fill in the information below.

THE UNITED STATES IN 1790

Total Population:	
Rural/Urban Distribution	

This important date in American history is brought to you by

_____

Shade and label the United States in 1803 on the map below. In a different color, shade and label the land acquired in the Louisiana Purchase. Then, complete the chart.

THE LOUISIANA PURCHASE

Area of Territory	
Acquired From	
How It Was Acquired	
Current States in Territory	

This important date in American history is brought to you by

_____

★1800

•1810

•1820

•1830

•1840

•1850

•1860

•1870

•1880

•1890

•1900

•1900

•1890

•1880

•1870

•1860

•1850

•1840

•1830

•1820

•1810

•1800

★1804–1806★

The Lewis and Clark Expedition

Study the illustration below. Then, write a caption for it that tells about the Lewis and Clark expedition. Your caption should tell what the Lewis and Clark expedition was and where it went.

_____

_____

_____

_____

This important date in American history is brought to you by

_____

Answer the questions below.

THE WOMAN

When did she live? _____

What was her nationality? _____

What did her name mean? _____

What do we know about her family? _____

_____

What words would you use to describe her? _____

_____

THE GUIDE AND INTERPRETER

In what specific ways did she help the expedition?

_____

_____

_____

_____

THE HISTORICAL FIGURE

How is Sacagawea honored today? _____

_____

This important date in American history is brought to you by

_____

Shade and label the United States in 1818 on the map below. Shade and label the Florida Cession. Then, complete the chart.

THE FLORIDA CESSION (1819)

Area of Territory	
Acquired From	
How It Was Acquired	
Current States in Territory	

This important date in American history is brought to you by

_____

Complete the chart below.

MANIFEST DESTINY

What the Idea Means	
Examples of the Idea in Action	
How the Idea Affected Americans	
How the Idea Affected Native Americans	

Rewrite the passage below in your own words.

"Our manifest destiny [is] to overspread the continent allotted by Providence for the free development of our yearly multiplying millions."

—John L. O'Sullivan, newspaper writer, 1845

_____

_____

_____

_____

_____

_____

This important date in American history is brought to you by

_____

★1843★ The Oregon Trail

Settlers first used the Oregon Trail in the 1830s. It was 1843, however, when the first large wagon train followed the Oregon Trail west. In this year, the "Great Migration" of about 1,000 settlers headed to "Oregon Country." Thousands more would follow.

THE OREGON TRAIL: NUMBERS TELL THE STORY

Length of Trail

Number of Settlers Who Used the Trail

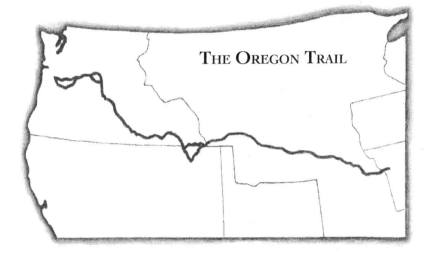

THE OREGON TRAIL

Average Time It Took
to Travel the Trail

Years the Trail
Was Used

Percentage of People Who
Survived the Trail

This important date in American history is brought to you by

_____

Shade and label the United States in 1845 on the map below. Shade and label the Texas Annexation. Then, complete the chart.

THE TEXAS ANNEXATION

Area of Territory	
Acquired From	
How It Was Acquired	
Current States in Territory	

This important date in American history is brought to you by

_____

Shade and label the United States in 1846 on the map below. Shade and label the Oregon Country Cession. Then, complete the chart.

THE OREGON COUNTRY CESSION

Area of Territory	
Acquired From	
How It Was Acquired	
Current States in Territory	

This important date in American history is brought to you by

_____

1800
1810
1820
1830
1840
1850
1860
1870
1880
1890
1900

1900
1890
1880
1870
1860
1850
1840
1830
1820
1810
1800

★1848★ The Mexican Cession

Shade and label the United States in 1848 on the map below. Shade and label the Mexican Cession. Then, complete the chart.

THE MEXICAN CESSION

Area of Territory	
Acquired From	
How It Was Acquired	
Current States in Territory	

This important date in American history is brought to you by

_____

Complete the diagram below.

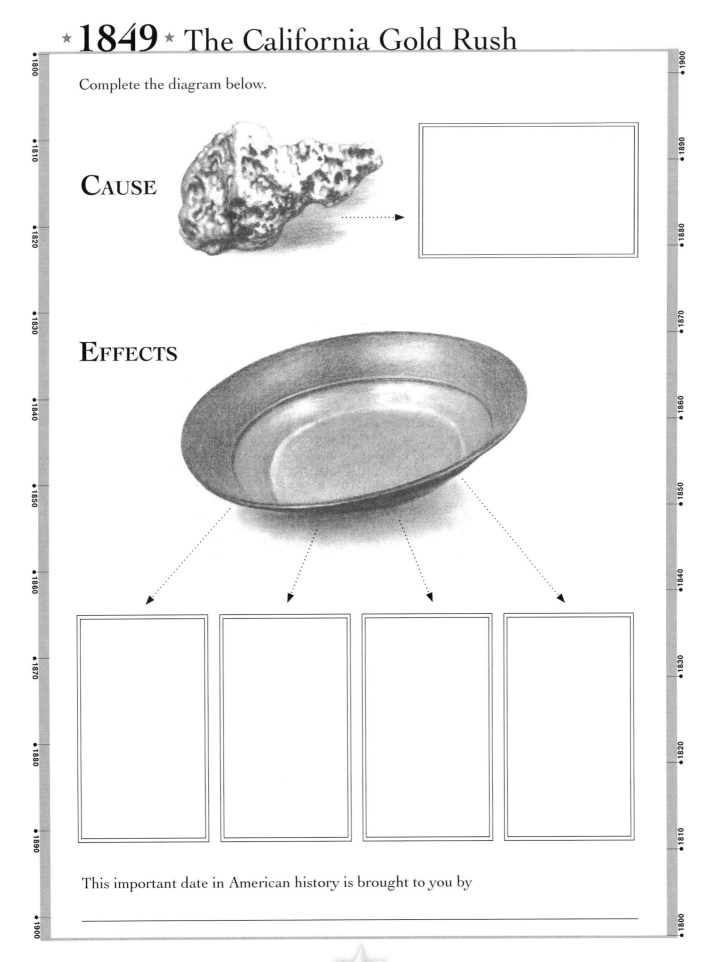

CAUSE

EFFECTS

This important date in American history is brought to you by

_____

During the Gold Rush

The discovery of gold turned San Francisco into a boomtown. Read how one man described it. Then answer the questions.

"There was no such thing as a home to be found. Scarcely even a proper house could be seen. Both dwellings and places of business were either common canvas tents or small, rough-board shanties or frame buildings of one story....

Nobody troubled himself to remove any rubbish from the way....

In those miserable apologies for houses, surrounded by heaps and patches of filth, mud, and stagnant water, the strange, mixed population carried on business....

All things seemed in the utmost disorder. The streets and passages, such as they were, and the inside of tents and houses were heaped with all sorts of goods and lumber. There seemed to be no method in anything. People bustled and jostled against each other, bawled, railed, and fought, cursed and swore, sweated and labored...and somehow work was done....

The whole population was constantly moving and always visible....

In order to accumulate the greatest heap of gold in the shortest possible time, schemes and actions had often to be resorted to which nice honor could not justify nor strict honesty adopt."

—Frank Soulé

What adjectives would you use to describe San Francisco during the gold rush?

_____

_____

Would you have liked to visit San Francisco during the gold rush? Why or why not?

_____

_____

This important date in American history is brought to you by

_____

Complete the chart below.

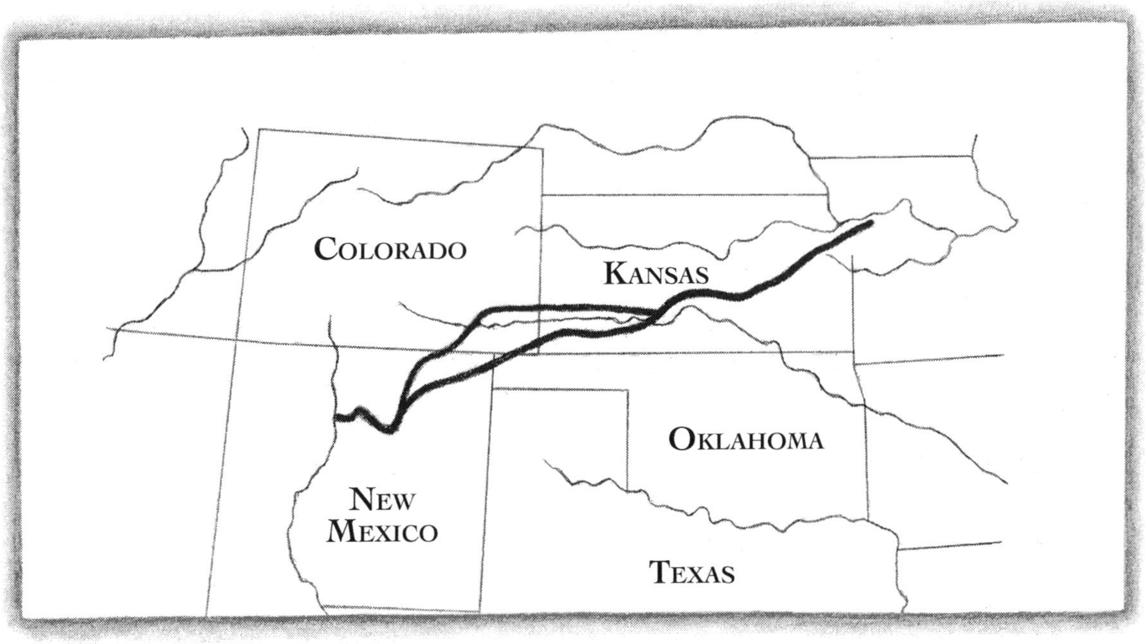

THE SANTE FE TRAIL

Where It Began	
Where It Ended	
Length of Trail	
Years It Was Used	
Why It Was Important to Traders	

This important date in American history is brought to you by

_____

★ **1800**
★ **1810**
★ **1820**
★ **1830**
★ **1840**
★ **1850**
★ **1860**
★ **1870**
★ **1880**
★ **1890**
★ **1900**

★ 1853 ★ The Gadsden Purchase

Shade and label the United States in 1853 on the map below. Shade and label the Gadsden Purchase. Then, complete the chart.

THE GADSDEN PURCHASE

Area of Territory	
Acquired From	
How It Was Acquired	
Current States in Territory	

This important date in American history is brought to you by

_____

Label the following items on the map below: states in 1860, several major cities, and major bodies of water.

Fill in the missing information below. Record the total population, and shade the circle graph to illustrate the rural/urban distribution.

THE UNITED STATES IN **1860**

Total Population: _____

Rural/Urban Distribution: _____

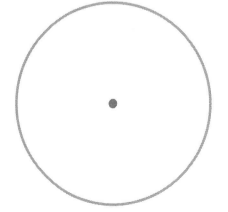

This important date in American history is brought to you by

_____

Activate the Time Machine to learn about entertainment during the first half of the 1800s. In the left-hand circle, write facts about entertainment during that time. In the right-hand circle, write facts about entertainment today. In the space where the circles overlap, write facts about entertainment that both time periods have in common.

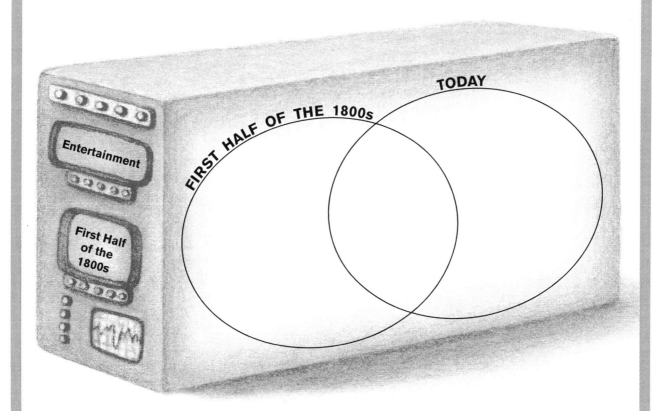

Most Americans in the first half of the 1800s spent a lot of their time working, so there was little time for leisure. Still, people found many ways to entertain themselves.

At home, families spent time visiting and telling stories. Children often made up games to play outside. New printing techniques made books and newspapers affordable, so reading was an important pastime.

Public gatherings were also important. Rural Americans went to local dances, socials, and fairs. For many people, church was an important social event. In the cities, plays were very popular.

This important trip into American history is brought to you by

_____

★ The Santa Fe National Historic Trail ★

The Santa Fe National Historic Trail is not a single location. It consists of dozens of locations along the route of the original Santa Fe Trail. What is it like to visit them? Conduct research to find out.

Use the Internet or any other resources your teacher suggests. Read the articles, and study the illustrations. When you have gathered enough information, make a postcard.

On the front of the postcard, draw a picture or attach a picture from a magazine or the Internet that gives some information about one of the sites along the Santa Fe National Historic Trail. On the back of the postcard, write a caption that explains the picture. Then, write a note to a friend that tells about things to do and see at the site.

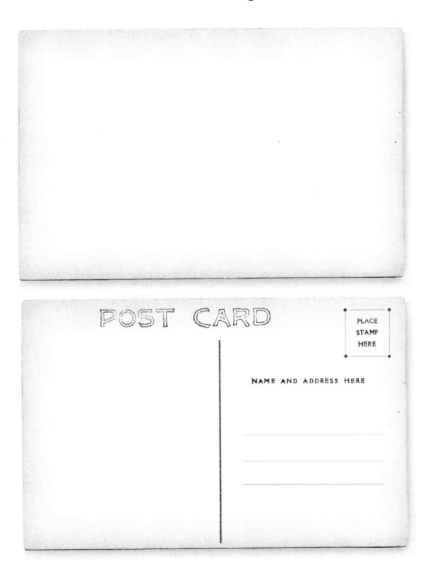

POST CARD

PLACE STAMP HERE

NAME AND ADDRESS HERE

This important place in American history is brought to you by

UNIT 6   An Age of Advancements   ★ TEACHING NOTES ★

1790–1860

UNIT OVERVIEW

The first half of the nineteenth century was a period of remarkable change in the United States. Unit 5 focused on the territorial growth of the country during this period. This unit is divided into three main sections that focus on the dramatic advances in industry, agriculture, transportation, and communication that took place during this time. Unit 7 addresses the social developments during this age of advancements.

Activity Sheet 6-A provides a unit overview. Activity Sheets 6-B through 6-E are concerned with the development of industry, focusing on mass production, the steam engine, and the Industrial Revolution (using Lowell as the model), as well as the effects of industry on working people. This section concludes with an overview of industry in the United States on the eve of the Civil War (Activity Sheet 6-F).

Activity Sheets 6-G through 6-I cover the development of agriculture, addressing three critical technological advancements—the cotton gin, the mechanical reaper, and the steel plow. This section concludes with an overview of agriculture in the United States on the eve of the Civil War (Activity Sheet 6-J).

Activity Sheets 6-K through 6-N focus on the development of transportation, including steamboats, roads, canals, and railroads. The key communication advancement of the time—the telegraph—is the focus of Activity Sheet 6-O. This section concludes with an overview of transportation and communication in the United States on the eve of the Civil War (Activity Sheet 6-P).

The Time Machine Activity, Activity Sheet 6-Q, compares communication today to communication during the first half of the nineteenth century. A Postcard From the Past, Activity 6-R, is about Lowell National Historical Park.

FOCUS ACTIVITIES

To focus the students' attention on this period of American history, consider the following activities:

Mass Production

Point to common objects in the classroom, and ask the students to explain how these objects were manufactured. Explain that most things were made in factories. Discuss how mass production works, including the need for power, machines, and interchangeable parts. Explain that this unit addresses how modern industry, which shapes people's lives every day, developed.

Changing the World

Ask the students what inventions or innovations of their time have reshaped the world (for example, computers and cell phones). Explain that many things were invented during the nineteenth century that changed people's lives in a major way, possibly even more drastically.

On the Farm

Invite a student to tell the class what vegetables he or she ate for lunch. Guide the students backwards to the origin of the meal—from the cafeteria to the food distributor's refrigerated delivery truck to the food processing plant to the farm. Emphasize the vital importance of agriculture to American civilization. Explain that some agricultural tools that seem to be simple inventions today were truly revolutionary when they were invented.

CONSTRUCTING THE TIMELINE

This unit consists of 18 activity sheets that focus on significant events, people, and places related to the important industrial, agricultural, transportation, and communication developments during the first half of the nineteenth century. Each activity sheet is designed to, once completed, become part of a posted classroom timeline of the period covered in the unit.

The Introduction (pages VII–XVI) provides a detailed explanation of how to use the activity sheets in the classroom and suggests various ways to construct the timeline using the completed activity sheets.

You can construct the timeline any way you see fit. Use the Timeline Components (pages XVIII–XXVI) to connect the activity sheets. Below are two possible timelines, constructed from the activity sheets in this unit and the Timeline Components.

Please note that the timeline for this unit can incorporate the subheadings provided on page XXV.

Option 1: Basic Timeline

Construct this timeline to identify only the essential elements of the period.

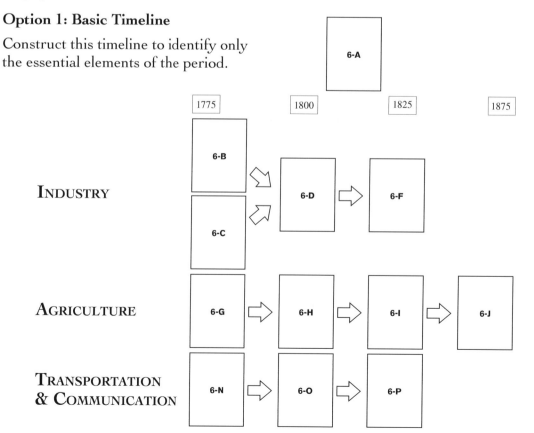

Option 2: Complete Timeline

Construct this timeline to identify the essential elements of the period, examine them in greater detail, and extend student learning.

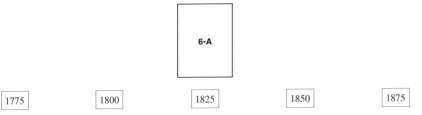

| 6-A |

| 1775 | 1800 | 1825 | 1850 | 1875 |

INDUSTRY

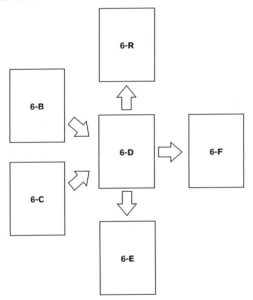

AGRICULTURE

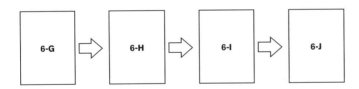

TRANSPORTATION & COMMUNICATION

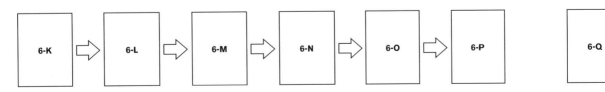

CRITICAL THINKING SKILLS

The activity sheets in this unit address various critical thinking skills. In addition, the constructed timeline emphasizes the essential critical thinking skills of identifying main ideas and details, sequencing events, and relating causes and effects.

Identifying Main Ideas and Details

Point out that Activity Sheet 6-A outlines the main ideas of the unit. Explain that the topics of the other activity sheets in the unit reflect the main ideas of the historical period the students are studying. Further explain that some activity sheets focus on the details related to specific topics.

As you and the students construct the timeline, show them that Activity Sheet 6-D forms a main idea and Activity Sheets 6-E and 6-R focus on details. Have the students annotate the Timeline Arrows appropriately. Challenge the students to find similar relationships or create them by rearranging the activity sheets.

Sequencing Events

Point out that the activity sheets that make up the timeline are sequential. Show the students how the Timeline Dates provide a concrete reference for when events happened and how they relate to other events. (For example, the mechanical reaper was invented in 1831 before the steel plow in 1837.) Make sure the students see that the Timeline Arrows indicate a chronological flow from left to right. Also, point out that this unit's timeline has three basic layers that are separated by subheadings.

As you and the students construct the timeline, show them that Activity Sheets 6-G through 6-I and Activity Sheets 6-K through 6-O feature developments that happened sequentially. Have the students annotate the Timeline Arrows appropriately. Challenge the students to find similar relationships or create them by rearranging the activity sheets.

Relating Causes and Effects

As you and the students construct the timeline, show them that Activity Sheets 6-B through 6-E form the causes of the effect addressed on Activity Sheet 6-F. Point out the similar relationships among Activity Sheets 6-G through 6-I (causes) and Activity Sheet 6-J (effect) as well as Activity Sheets 6-K through 6-O (causes) and Activity Sheet 6-P (effect). Have the students annotate the Timeline Arrows appropriately. Challenge the students to find similar relationships or create them by rearranging the activity sheets.

INDIVIDUAL ACTIVITY SHEET NOTES

The following notes provide a variety of tips on how to guide the students through the completion and extension of each activity sheet.

6-A. An Age of Advancements

This activity is most appropriate for the students to complete with partners, in small groups, or as a whole class. For example, you might want to complete the questions with the whole class at the beginning of the unit and then have the students answer the questions at the end of the unit. Encourage the students to think of additional questions related to the topic.

6-B. Biography: Eli Whitney

The focus of this activity is not the cotton gin but rather Whitney's promotion of the interchangeable system—the use of interchangeable parts in the manufacturing process, an essential element of mass production. The date of 1798 is selected because that is the year Whitney received his contract to manufacture muskets for the federal government.

6-C. The Steam Engine

The date of 1800 is selected because that is the year Evans began work on a successful high-pressure steam engine. Emphasize the importance of steam in powering a wide variety of manufacturing and transportation technologies.

6-D. Lowell and the Industrial Revolution

Present the Industrial Revolution as one of the most dramatic and fundamental shifts in human history. Explain the origin of the Industrial Revolution in England as well as in the textile industry. Point out that the United States was the first country outside of Europe to industrialize.

6-E. A Voice From the Past: Life in a Factory Town

Point out that most of the workers at Lowell were young girls—the famous "mill girls." Have the students compare and contrast working conditions then and working conditions today. Ask the students how the labor movement is responsible for the improvements.

6-F. American Industry in 1860

Emphasize that industry grew dramatically during the first half of the nineteenth century.

6-G. Eli Whitney's Cotton Gin

If possible, provide raw cotton bolls to give the students a sense of how difficult and time-consuming it was to pick cotton by hand. Explain that the cotton gin made cotton production and profits skyrocket, actually increasing the demand for slaves even though it was a labor-saving device.

6-H. Cyrus McCormick's Mechanical Reaper

To give the students a sense of how revolutionary the mechanical reaper was, explain that two men operating a reaper could cut as much grain in one day as 16 men working with scythes.

6-I. John Deere's Plow

Make sure the students understand the key features of Deere's plow. Explain that earlier plows were designed for the sandy soil of the eastern United States. These plows could not cut the tough prairie sod of the western United States. The plows quickly became so coated with soil that they clogged up and had to be cleaned. Deere's plow could tackle the sod and was self-cleaning.

6-J. American Agriculture in 1860

Emphasize that agriculture grew dramatically during the first half of the nineteenth century.

6-K. The *Clermont*

Point out that steamboats were fast and could travel upstream. They made transportation of goods easier and much more economical. By 1855, more than 700 steamboats plowed American waterways and brought goods and people to and from locations on the Mississippi, Ohio, Missouri, Red, and Arkansas Rivers.

6-L. The National Road

Explain that the early 1800s were glory days for turnpikes and plank roads but that the road system declined by 1850. It suffered from competition from steamboats, canal barges, and railroads.

6-M. Map Study: The Erie Canal

Tell the students that the great period of canal building lasted from 1825, when the Erie Canal was completed, to 1840. By that time, there were more than 3,300 miles of canals in the United States.

6-N. The Railroads

Make sure the students graph the data properly and draw the correct conclusions about the expansion and usefulness of the railroads. Discuss how this technology would affect the economy and the growth of the country.

6-O. The Telegraph

Discuss how revolutionary this technology truly was. Compare this form of communication to the telephone today. Ask the students how much of a difference not having a telephone would make in their everyday lives.

6-P. American Transportation and Communication in 1860

Emphasize the growth of the population during the first half of the nineteenth century and the beginning of the shift from a rural to an urban country.

6-Q. The Time Machine: Communication

Help the students identify the main points of the essay, which should be written in the left-hand circle of the Venn diagram.

6-R: A Postcard From the Past: Lowell National Historical Park

Suggest that the students visit www.nps.gov (the web site of the National Park Service) to gather information about Lowell National Historical Park.

An Age of Advancements

In the box below, draw a picture or attach a picture from a magazine or the Internet that represents this period of American history. The picture can be of anything you think is appropriate.

Ask questions about this period of American history. Then, answer them.

Question: WHO_____?

Answer:_____

Question: WHAT_____?

Answer:_____

Question: WHERE _____?

Answer:_____

Question: WHEN _____?

Answer:_____

Question: WHY _____?

Answer:_____

Question: HOW_____?

Answer:_____

This important date in American history is brought to you by

_____

Answer the questions below.

THE MAN

When did he live? _____

What do we know about his early life? _____

_____

_____

_____

What words would you use to describe him? _____

_____

_____

HIS CONTRIBUTIONS

What was the interchangeable system? _____

_____

_____

What did Whitney use interchangeable parts to make? _____

_____

Why are interchangeable parts important for mass production? _____

_____

_____

This important date in American history is brought to you by

_____

Complete the diagram below.

How It Was Important
to Industrialization

How It Was Important
to Transportation

The Contributions
of Oliver Evans

This important date in American history is brought to you by

_____

★1822★ Lowell and the Industrial Revolution

The industrial city of Lowell, Massachusetts, was founded in 1822. A historian wrote, "While there is no single birthplace of industry, [Francis Cabot] Lowell's planned textile mill city, in scale, technological innovation, and development of an urban working class, marked the beginning of the industrial transformation of America."

Answer the following questions about "the industrial transformation of America."

What was the Industrial Revolution?

_____

_____

_____

_____

_____

When did the Industrial Revolution in America take place?_____

Where in the United States was most industry located in the first half of the 1800s?

_____

How did the Industrial Revolution change life in the United States? _____

_____

_____

Why is the Industrial Revolution important?_____

_____

This important date in American history is brought to you by

_____

Visitors to Lowell made this report.

"We have lately visited the cities of Lowell and Manchester, and have had an opportunity of examining the factory system more closely than before....

In Lowell live between seven and eight thousand young women, who are generally daughters of farmers of the different States of New England....

The operatives work thirteen hours a day in the summer time, and from daylight to dark in the winter. At half past four in the morning the factory bell rings, and at five the girls must be in the mills.... At seven the girls are allowed thirty minutes for breakfast, and at noon thirty minutes more for dinner.... But within this time they must hurry to their boarding-houses and return to the factory, and that through the hot sun, or the rain and cold.... At seven o'clock in the evening the factory bell sounds the close of the day's work."

What words would you use to describe life in Lowell? _____

_____

_____

_____

Do you think the factory owners treated the workers fairly? Why or why not? _____

_____

_____

_____

This important date in American history is brought to you by

_____

Complete the page.

AMERICAN INDUSTRY IN 1860

How It Was Different
From Industry in 1800

_____

_____

_____

_____

_____

_____

_____

_____

Location of Most Industries _____

_____

Effects of Industry on Workers _____

_____

_____

Effects of Industry on Economy _____

_____

_____

This important date in American history is brought to you by

_____

Complete the page.

"One man and a horse [driving the cotton gin] will do more than fifty men with the old machines."

—Eli Whitney

What It Did _____

_____

How It Affected Agriculture in the South _____

_____

_____

How It Affected Enslaved African Americans_____

_____

_____

This important date in American history is brought to you by

_____

1800
1810
1820
1830
1840
1850
1860
1870
1880
1890
1900

★ 1831 ★ Cyrus McCormick's Mechanical Reaper

Answer the questions below.

THE MECHANICAL REAPER

What did the mechanical reaper do? _____

_____

How did it contribute to agriculture? _____

_____

How did it contribute to American expansion into the plains? _____

_____

How did it affect the number of farm workers needed? _____

_____

This important date in American history is brought to you by

_____

1900
1890
1880
1870
1860
1850
1840
1830
1820
1810
1800

Use the words in the box below to label the illustration. Then, answer the questions.

handles	moldboard	share	beam	hitch

What made John Deere's plow different from earlier ones? _____

_____

Why was his plow needed to farm the prairie and plains? _____

_____

How did his plow contribute to America's westward expansion? _____

_____

This important date in American history is brought to you by

_____

Complete the page.

AMERICAN AGRICULTURE IN 1860

How It Was Different From Agriculture in 1800 _____

_____

Major Crops _____

_____

Location of Most Farms _____

_____

Effects of Agriculture on Economy_____

_____

This important date in American history is brought to you by

_____

★ 1807 ★ The *Clermont*

Study the illustration below. Then, write a caption for it that tells about the *Clermont*. Your caption should tell what the *Clermont* was, where it ran, who built it, and why it was important.

1800
1810
1820
1830
1840
1850
1860
1870
1880
1890
1900

1900
1890
1880
1870
1860
1850
1840
1830
1820
1810
1800

_____

_____

_____

_____

_____

_____

This important date in American history is brought to you by

_____

★ 1811 ★ The National Road

Construction on the National Road began in 1811. Write five important facts about it beside the "road" below. Then, answer the question.

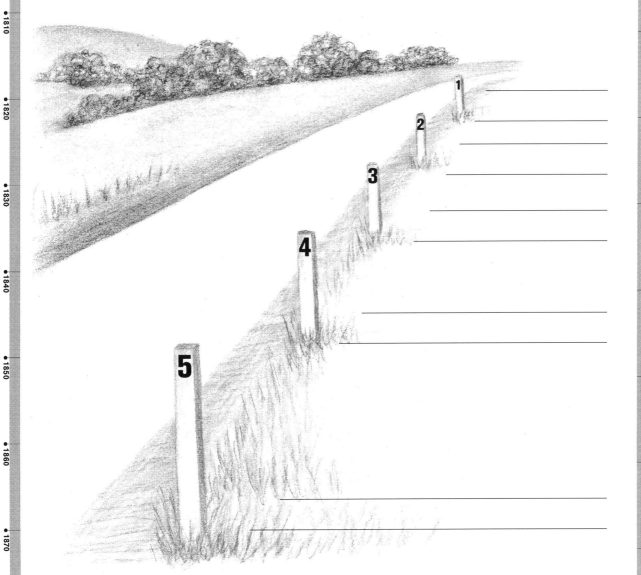

What was an important effect of the increase in road construction during the early 1800s?

_____

_____

This important date in American history is brought to you by

_____

Label the following items on the map below: Lake Erie and Lake Ontario; New York State; the cities of Troy, Rome, and Buffalo; the Hudson River; and the Erie Canal.

Answer the questions below.

Why was the Erie Canal built? _____

_____

What did it connect? _____

How long was the Erie Canal? _____

How did people travel on the Erie Canal? _____

Why was the Erie Canal important?_____

_____

This important date in American history is brought to you by

_____

Answer the questions below.

MILES OF RAILROAD TRACK IN THE UNITED STATES, 1800–1860

Year	Approximate Miles of Railroad Track
1800	0
1810	0
1820	0
1830	23
1840	3,000
1850	9,000
1860	30,000

What conclusions can you draw from the chart? _____

_____

_____

_____

How did the growth of the railroad system from 1830 to 1860 affect the United States?

_____

_____

_____

This important date in American history is brought to you by

_____

Complete the fact sheet below.

FACT SHEET: THE TELEGRAPH

What It Was: _____

How It Worked: _____

_____

_____

Who Invented It: _____

Effects of Its Invention: _____

_____

_____

_____

This important date in American history is brought to you by

_____

and Communication

Complete the page.

TRANSPORTATION

How It Was Different From Transportation in 1800

_____

_____

Major Methods of Transportation_____

_____

Effects of Improved Transportation _____

_____

_____

COMMUNICATION

How It Was Different From Communication in 1800 _____

_____

Major Methods of Communication_____

_____

Effects of Improved Communication _____

_____

_____

This important date in American history is brought to you by

_____

Activate the Time Machine to learn about communication during the first half of the 1800s. In the left-hand circle, write facts about communication during that time. In the right-hand circle, write facts about communication today. In the space where the circles overlap, write facts about communication that both time periods have in common.

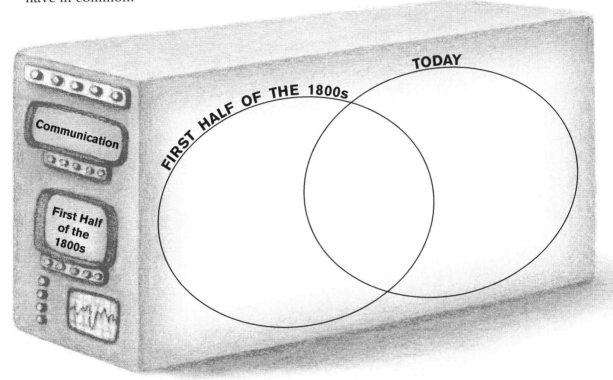

In 1800, there were about 900 post offices in the United States. By 1850, that number had jumped—with the growing population and its movement westward—to about 18,000. Still, mail was expensive. The person receiving the letter had to pay postage. People did not use envelopes, so the letters weren't private. The mail was also slow; typically, it took weeks—or longer—for a letter to reach another city.

Communication took a great leap forward during the 1840s with the expansion of the telegraph. This meant that distance would no longer slow communication. The "lightning line" made communication nearly instantaneous. By 1860, there were tens of thousands of miles of telegraph wires. Soon, nearly every town had a telegraph office.

The first half of the 1800s also saw great growth in the print industry. In 1800, there were about 20 daily newspapers in the country. By 1860, that number had soared to almost 400. Magazine and book publishers grew too. By the 1840s, many magazines, printed in New York or Boston, had readers all over the country. This "print explosion" followed the pioneers west. New settlements often included a print shop, set up by pioneer printers who knew the American people always hungered for something to read.

This important trip into American history is brought to you by

★Lowell National Historical Park★

Lowell, Massachusetts, was the first truly industrial city in the United States. It was the birthplace of the American Industrial Revolution. Today, much of the city's industrial heritage is preserved at Lowell National Historical Park. What is it like to visit there? Conduct research to find out.

Use the Internet or any other resources your teacher suggests. Read the articles, and study the illustrations. When you have gathered enough information, make a postcard.

On the front of the postcard, draw a picture or attach a picture from a magazine or the Internet that gives some information about Lowell National Historical Park. On the back of the postcard, write a caption that explains the picture. Then, write a note to a friend that tells about things to do and see at the park.

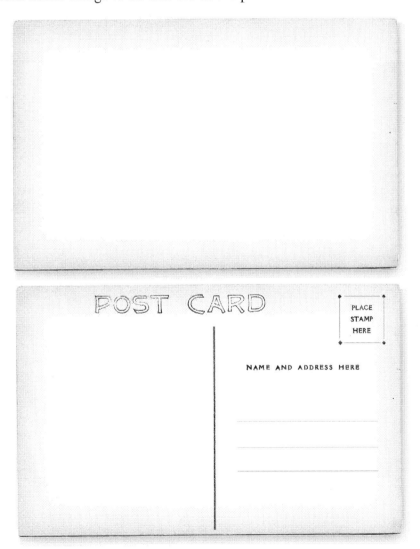

POST CARD

PLACE
STAMP
HERE

NAME AND ADDRESS HERE

This important place in American history is brought to you by

UNIT 7   Social Issues

1790–1860

UNIT OVERVIEW

The United States experienced an incredible period of growth and change during the first half of the nineteenth century. This unit focuses on the major social issues of the time: conflicts with Native Americans, women's rights, and slavery.

Activity Sheet 7-A provides a unit overview. Activity Sheets 7-B through 7-E are concerned with the effects of American expansion on Native Americans, specifically the effects of the Indian Removal Act, notably the Trail of Tears, and the Seminole War.

Activity Sheets 7-F through 7-I focus on the burgeoning women's rights movement of this time, especially the fight for suffrage. Specifically, students examine the Seneca Falls convention and learn about Elizabeth Cady Stanton and her comrade Frederick Douglass. This pairing represents the link between the two main social movements of the period—women's rights and abolition—as does Activity Sheet 7-I, which quotes Sojourner Truth's most famous speech.

Activity Sheets 7-J through 7-M address slavery and the movement to abolish it. This section begins with an overview of slavery in the United States and further explores the Missouri Compromise, the abolitionist movement, and the Underground Railroad.

The Time Machine Activity, Activity Sheet 7-N, compares music today to music during the first half of the nineteenth century. A Postcard From the Past, Activity Sheet 7-O, is about the John Rankin House, an important center of abolitionist activity.

FOCUS ACTIVITIES

To focus the students' attention on this period of American history, consider the following activities:

The Cost of Manifest Destiny

Invite the students to list adjectives and phrases that describe the effects the growth of the United States had on Native Americans. Point out that these descriptions are usually negative, and remind the students that the United States grew at the expense of many groups of people. Explain that the new nation that was replacing the Native American nations faced serious social issues itself.

All Men Are Created Equal

Remind the students of the famous "truth" in the Declaration of Independence that states, "All men are created equal." Ask the students if they would have signed the Declaration of Independence. Point out that today, some Americans think the phrase should state, "All men and women are created equal," and that many women in the nineteenth century felt the same way. Ask the students how they think the phrase should be worded.

American Heroes

Invite the students to share what they know about the Underground Railroad. Ask them what makes someone a hero. Discuss whether escaping slaves and the people who helped them should be considered heroes.

CONSTRUCTING THE TIMELINE

This unit consists of 15 activity sheets that focus on significant events, people, and places related to the major social issues during the first half of the nineteenth century. Each activity sheet is designed to, once completed, become part of a posted classroom timeline of the period covered in the unit.

The Introduction (pages VII–XVI) provides a detailed explanation of how to use the activity sheets in the classroom and suggests various ways to construct the timeline using the completed activity sheets.

You can construct the timeline any way you see fit. Use the Timeline Components (pages XVIII–XXVI) to connect the activity sheets. Below are two possible timelines, constructed from the activity sheets in this unit and the Timeline Components.

Please note that the timeline for this unit can incorporate the subheadings provided on page XXVI.

Option 1: Basic Timeline

Construct this timeline to identify only the essential elements of the period.

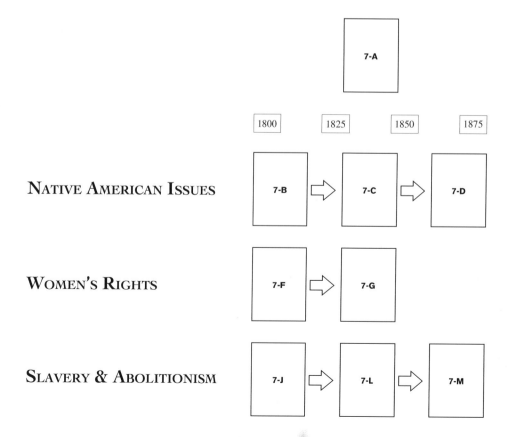

Option 2: Complete Timeline

Construct this timeline to identify the essential elements of the period, examine them in greater detail, and extend student learning.

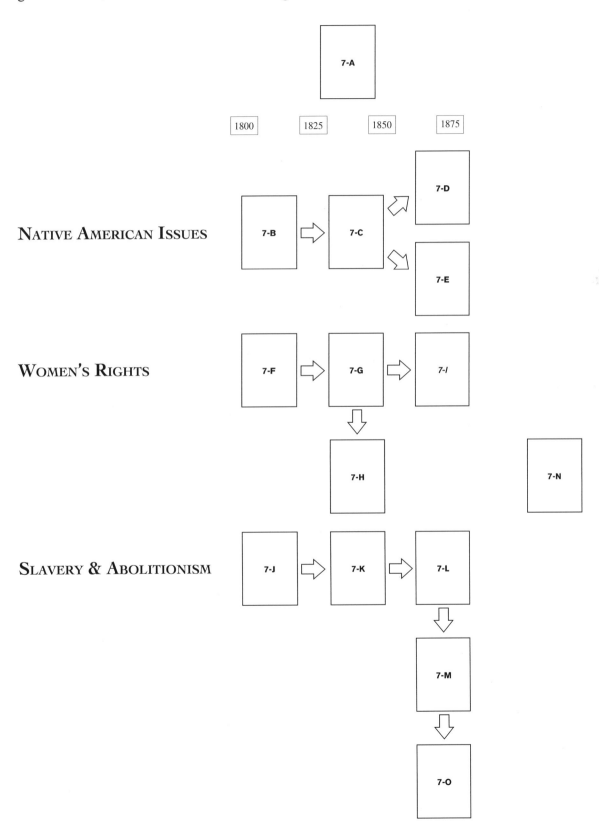

CRITICAL THINKING SKILLS

The activity sheets in this unit address various critical thinking skills. In addition, the constructed timeline emphasizes the essential critical thinking skills of identifying main ideas and details, sequencing events, and relating causes and effects.

Identifying Main Ideas and Details

Point out that Activity Sheet 7-A outlines the main ideas of the unit. Explain that the topics of the other activity sheets in the unit reflect the main ideas of the historical period the students are studying. Further explain that some activity sheets focus on the details related to specific topics.

As you and the students construct the timeline, show them that Activity Sheet 7-G forms a main idea and Activity Sheet 7-H focuses on details. Point out the similar relationships among Activity Sheet 7-L (main idea) and Activity Sheets 7-M and 7-O (details). Have the students annotate the Timeline Arrows appropriately. Challenge the students to find similar relationships or create them by rearranging the activity sheets.

Sequencing Events

Point out that the activity sheets that make up the timeline are sequential. Show the students how the Timeline Dates provide a concrete reference for when events happened and how they relate to other events. (For example, the Indian Removal Act happened in 1830 before the Seminole War in 1835.) Make sure the students see that the Timeline Arrows indicate a chronological flow from left to right. Also, point out that this unit's timeline has three basic layers that are separated by subheadings.

Relating Causes and Effects

As you and the students construct the timeline, show them that the following activity sheets form a cause/effect relationship: 7-C/7-D, 7-C/7-E, and 7-L/7-M. Have the students annotate the Timeline Arrows appropriately. Challenge the students to find similar relationships or create them by rearranging the activity sheets.

INDIVIDUAL ACTIVITY SHEET NOTES

The notes below provide a variety of tips on how to guide the students through the completion and extension of each activity sheet.

7-A. Social Issues

This activity is most appropriate for the students to complete with partners, in small groups, or as a whole class. For example, you might want to complete the questions with the whole class at the beginning of the unit and then have the students answer the questions at the end of the unit. Encourage the students to think of additional questions related to the topic.

7-B. Expansion and Native Americans

Instruct the students to list facts about the effects America's westward expansion had on Native Americans.

7-C. The Indian Removal Act

Discuss the role Andrew Jackson played in the displacement of native peoples, both before and during his presidency.

7-D. The Trail of Tears

Make sure the students understand that there were actually several different Trails of Tears, involving different Native American nations.

7-E. The Seminole War

Emphasize the remarkable, steadfast resistance of the Seminole people. Explain that even today this resistance serves as the basis for lawsuits against the federal government.

7-F. Women's Rights

Instruct the students to list significant facts about the women's rights and suffrage movements of the time.

7-G. The Seneca Falls Convention

Tell the students that the location of the convention is honored today in Women's Rights National Historical Park. Invite interested students to learn more about the park and share what they learn with the class.

7-H. Biography: Elizabeth Cady Stanton and Frederick Douglass

Explain the cooperation and sympathy that existed between members of the women's rights and abolition movements (although the members were often at odds over goals and techniques).

7-I. A Voice From the Past: Sojourner Truth

Make sure the students understand who Sojourner Truth was. Help them with any difficult vocabulary. Point out the use of archaic words and phrases. Make sure the students understand that Truth's use of the word "Negroes" was the accepted term for African Americans at that time and was not in the least bit disrespectful.

7-J. Slavery in the United States

Instruct the students to list significant facts about slavery in the United States. Suggest that the students include concrete figures (for example, the number of slaves in the United States), as well as other facts.

7-K. The Missouri Compromise

Make sure the students understand that the Missouri Compromise helped to lessen tensions in the United States.

7-L. The Abolitionist Movement

Point out that abolitionist leaders were both black and white and that the abolitionist movement was the most intense and controversial social issue of the time.

7-M. Map Study: The Underground Railroad

Inform the students that historians estimate that about 30,000 people escaped to freedom on the Underground Railroad. Explain that the Underground Railroad was not a formal, organized entity but rather a loose network. Give the students reading assignments about the remarkable exploits of Harriet Tubman.

7-N. The Time Machine: Music

Help the students identify the main points of the essay, which should be written in the left-hand circle of the Venn diagram.

7-O. A Postcard From the Past: John Rankin House National Historic Landmark

Suggest that the students visit www.nps.gov (the web site of the National Park Service) to gather information about the John Rankin House National Historic Landmark.

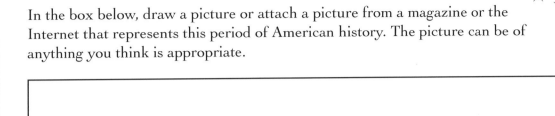
In the box below, draw a picture or attach a picture from a magazine or the Internet that represents this period of American history. The picture can be of anything you think is appropriate.

Ask questions about this period of American history. Then, answer them.

Question: WHO _____?

Answer: _____

Question: WHAT _____?

Answer: _____

Question: WHERE _____?

Answer: _____

Question: WHEN _____?

Answer: _____

Question: WHY _____?

Answer: _____

Question: HOW _____?

Answer: _____

This important date in American history is brought to you by

_____

Complete the sentence below. Then, complete the diagram by listing six important facts about America's westward expansion and Native Americans.

In 1824, the federal government established the Bureau of Indian Affairs. Its purpose

was to _____

_____ .

Expansion
and
Native
Americans

This important date in American history is brought to you by

_____

1800
1810
1820
1830
1840
1850
1860
1870
1880
1890
1900
1900
1890
1880
1870
1860
1850
1840
1830
1820
1810
1800

★1830★ The Indian Removal Act

Complete the diagram below by defining the Indian Removal Act and then describing it from each point of view.

THE INDIAN REMOVAL ACT

What It Did

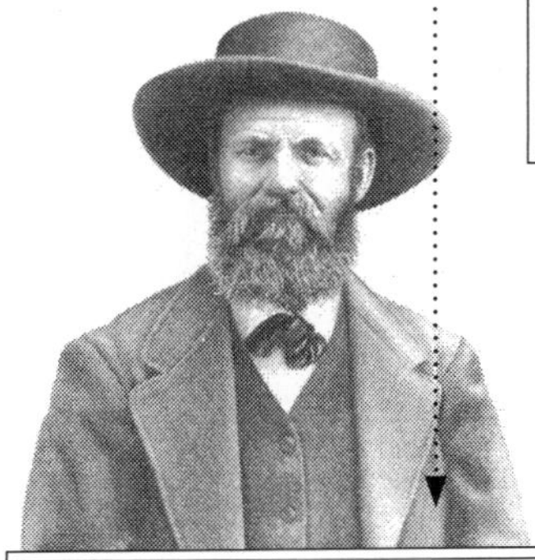

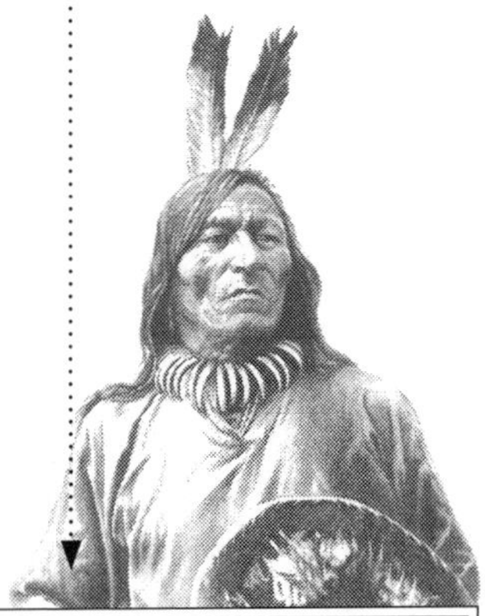

Description From Settlers' Point of View

Description From Native Americans' Point of View

This important date in American history is brought to you by

____

Study the illustration below. Then, write a caption for it that tells about the Trail of Tears. Your caption should tell what the Trail of Tears was, where it got its name, and why it happened.

_____

_____

_____

_____

_____

This important date in American history is brought to you by

_____

Complete the fact sheet below.

FACT SHEET: THE SEMINOLE WAR

What Caused It: _____

_____

_____

Who Fought It: _____

Results: _____

_____

_____

_____

This important date in American history is brought to you by

_____

Complete the sentence below. Then, complete the diagram by listing six important facts about women's rights.

In 1848, the first women's rights convention was held in Seneca Falls, New York. Its

purpose was to _____

_____ .

Women's Rights in the First Half of the 1800s

This important date in American history is brought to you by

_____

Complete the diagram below.

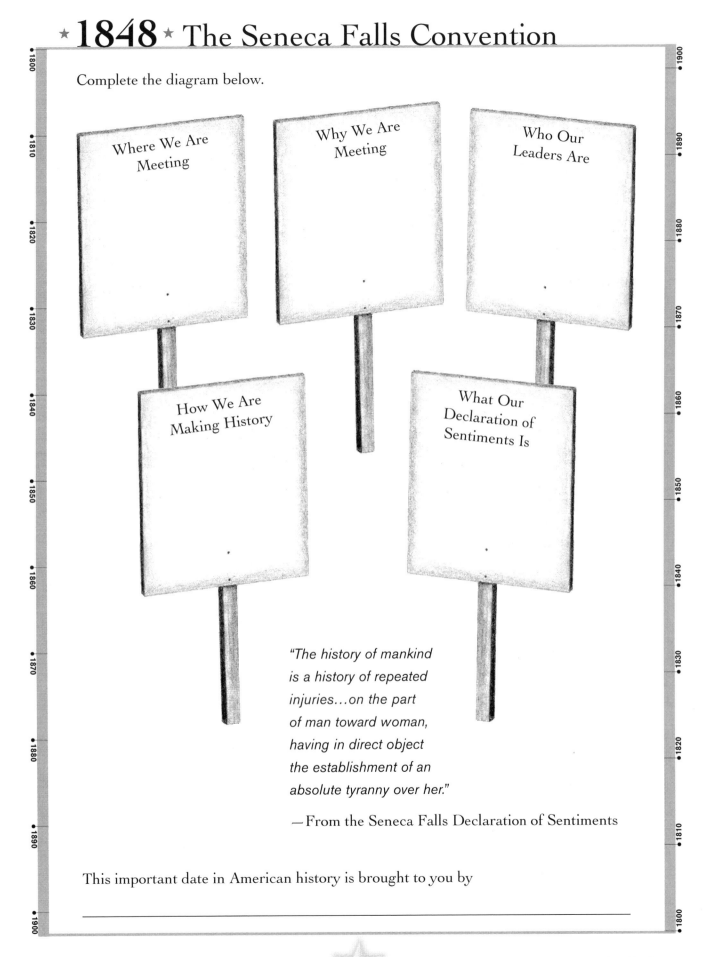

Where We Are Meeting

Why We Are Meeting

Who Our Leaders Are

How We Are Making History

What Our Declaration of Sentiments Is

"The history of mankind is a history of repeated injuries…on the part of man toward woman, having in direct object the establishment of an absolute tyranny over her."

—From the Seneca Falls Declaration of Sentiments

This important date in American history is brought to you by

_____

Answer the questions below.

ELIZABETH CADY STANTON

When did she live? _____

What contributions did she make to the women's rights

movement? _____

_____

_____

What words would you use to describe her? _____

_____

FREDERICK DOUGLASS

When did he live? _____

What contributions did he make to the abolitionist

movement? _____

_____

_____

What words would you use to describe him?

_____

What did Elizabeth Cady Stanton and Frederick Douglass have in common?

_____

This important date in American history is brought to you by

_____

Sojourner Truth was an African-American woman and a former slave. She became famous for the speeches she made against slavery. She also spoke on behalf of women. Read this excerpt from Sojourner Truth's "Ain't I a Woman" speech below. Then, answer the questions.

"That man over there says that women need to be helped into carriages, and lifted over ditches, and to have the best place everywhere. Nobody ever helps me into carriages, or over mud puddles, or gives me any best place! And ain't I a woman? Look at me! Look at my arm! I have ploughed, and planted, and gathered into barns, and no man could head me! And ain't I a woman? I could work as much and eat as much as a man—when I could get it—and bear the lash as well! And ain't I a woman? I have borne thirteen children, and seen most all sold off to slavery, and when I cried out with my mother's grief, none but Jesus heard me! And ain't I a woman?

Then they talk about this thing in the head; what's this they call it? ["Intellect," someone in the audience says.] That's it, honey. What's that got to do with women's rights or Negroes' rights? If my cup won't hold but a pint, and yours holds a quart, wouldn't you be mean not to let me have my little half-measure full?

Then that little man in black there, he says women can't have as much rights as men, 'cause Christ wasn't a woman! Where did your Christ come from? Where did your Christ come from? From God and a woman! Man had nothing to do with Him....

If the first woman God ever made was strong enough to turn the world upside down all alone, these women together ought to be able to turn it back, and get it right side up again! And now they is asking to do it, the men better let them.

Obliged to you for hearing me, and now old Sojourner hasn't got nothing more to say."

—Sojourner Truth

What is Sojourner Truth's main point? _____

_____

Does she do a good job of making her point? Explain. _____

_____

This important date in American history is brought to you by

_____

Complete the sentence below. Then, complete the diagram by listing six important facts about slavery in the United States.

In 1808, the slave trade was banned. This did not end slavery, though, because _____

_____ .

Slavery in the United States

This important date in American history is brought to you by

_____

Complete the diagram below.

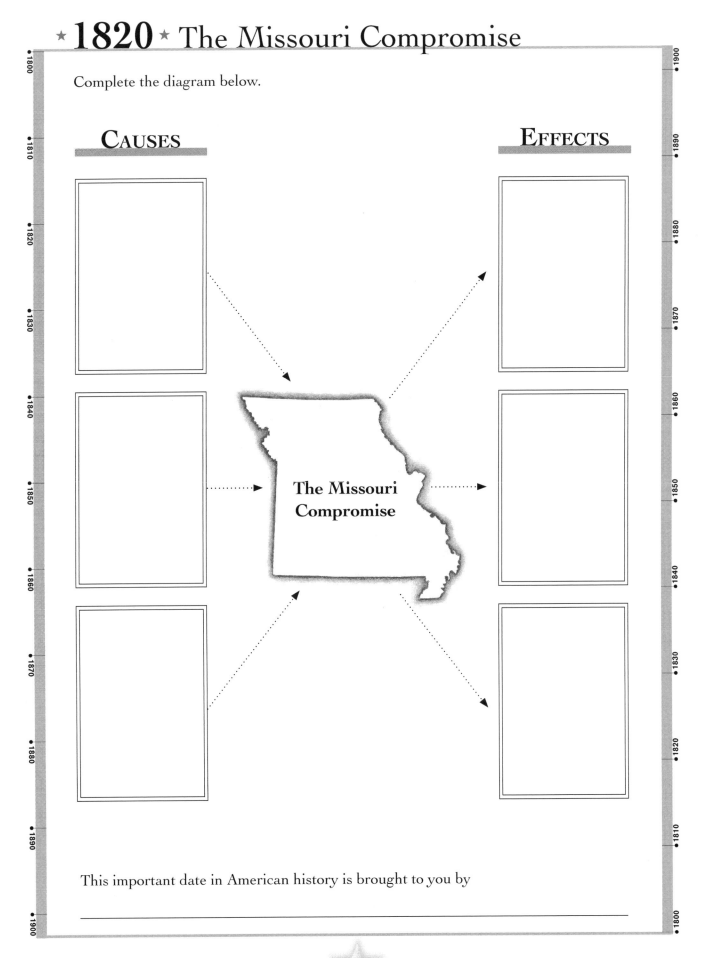

CAUSES

EFFECTS

The Missouri
Compromise

1800 1810 1820 1830 1840 1850 1860 1870 1880 1890 1900

1900 1890 1880 1870 1860 1850 1840 1830 1820 1810 1800

This important date in American history is brought to you by

_____

1800
1810
1820
1830
1840
1850
1860
1870
1880
1890
1900

1900
1890
1880
1870
1860
1850
1840
1830
1820
1810
1800

William Lloyd Garrison, a leading abolitionist, started his anti-slavery newspaper, *The Liberator*, in 1831. Garrison was unwavering in his opposition to slavery. He wrote, "I am in earnest; I will not equivocate; I will not excuse; I will not retreat a single inch; and I will be heard!"

Answer the questions about the abolitionist movement below.

What was abolitionism, or the abolition movement?

_____

_____

When did the abolition movement take place?

_____

Who were some leading abolitionists?

_____

_____

Where in the United States did most abolitionists live? _____

_____

How did abolitionists seek to accomplish their goals? _____

_____

_____

Why is the abolition movement important? _____

_____

_____

This important date in American history is brought to you by

_____

The Underground Railroad

Draw the Underground Railroad on the map below. Use arrows to indicate major routes on the Underground Railroad. Then, label important locations on the Underground Railroad. When you have completed the map, write a caption that tells about the Underground Railroad.

_____

_____

_____

_____

This important date in American history is brought to you by

_____

Activate the Time Machine to learn about music during the first half of the 1800s. In the left-hand circle, write facts about music during that time. In the right-hand circle, write facts about music today. In the space where the circles overlap, write facts about music that both time periods have in common.

Music was an important form of entertainment during this time. Many families sang songs together. A lot of people owned their own instruments. Wealthy families had pianos in their homes that they would gather around to sing.

Workers would sing or chant to help them get through their long days. Children would sing in school. Music was an important part of many religious services.

In the South, enslaved African Americans sang religious songs called spirituals. These songs helped ease the enslaved people's minds. Many times, though, the songs had a different purpose. The enslaved people used them to send messages to each other—messages their overseers couldn't understand. Some songs even taught the enslaved people how to escape to the North.

This important trip into American history is brought to you by

_____

★ John Rankin House
National Historic Landmark ★

John Rankin was an important abolitionist. His home was a "station" on the Underground Railroad. Today, the John Rankin House is preserved as a National Historic Landmark. What is it like to visit there? Conduct research to find out.

Use the Internet or any other resources your teacher suggests. Read the articles, and study the illustrations. When you have gathered enough information, make a postcard.

On the front of the postcard, draw a picture or attach a picture from a magazine or the Internet that gives some information about the John Rankin House. On the back of the postcard, write a caption that explains the picture. Then, write a note to a friend that tells about things to do and see at the house.

POST CARD

PLACE STAMP HERE

NAME AND ADDRESS HERE

This important place in American history is brought to you by

UNIT 8 The Civil War and Reconstruction

1850–1877

UNIT OVERVIEW

The Civil War began on April 12, 1861, with the firing on Fort Sumter, but the essential conflict between the North and South took root decades earlier. Some of these factors were covered in Units 5, 6, and 7. This unit focuses on the issues that brought the United States to the brink of war and then over the brink into the bloodiest conflict in the nation's history.

Activity Sheet 8-A provides a unit overview. Activity Sheet 8-B focuses on the Compromise of 1850, which temporarily cooled the growing heat of conflict. Activity Sheets 8-C and 8-D address two events that fanned the fires—the publication of *Uncle Tom's Cabin* and the Kansas-Nebraska Act.

Activity Sheet 8-E helps the students see that the divisions between the North and South went beyond the issue of slavery, and Activity Sheet 8-F illustrates the geopolitical consequences of that divide. Activity Sheet 8-G features a mini-timeline of the major events of the Civil War. Activity Sheets 8-H through 8-J emphasize the important role Abraham Lincoln played during this period of American history.

Activity Sheet 8-K is concerned with Reconstruction, which took place after the Civil War. Activity Sheet 8-L shows the country reunited, populous, and increasingly urban.

The Time Machine Activity, Activity Sheet 8-M, compares toys and games today to toys and games during the middle 1800s. A Postcard From the Past, Activity Sheet 8-N, is about Gettysburg National Military Park.

FOCUS ACTIVITIES

To focus the students' attention on this period of American history, consider the following activities:

The Deadliest War

Ask the students what they think the deadliest war in American history is. It might surprise them that the Civil War, with the death of about 620,000 soldiers, cost nearly as many lives as all of America's other wars combined.

"Four score and seven years ago…"

Give, or have a student give, a dramatic reading of the Gettysburg Address, provided on Activity Sheet 8-I. Use the questions on the activity sheet as a basis for class discussion.

Field Trip

Invite any students who have visited a Civil War battlefield to share their experiences with the class.

CONSTRUCTING THE TIMELINE

This unit consists of 14 activity sheets that focus on significant events, people, and places related to the Civil War period and Reconstruction. Each activity sheet is designed to, once completed, become part of a posted classroom timeline of the period.

The Introduction (pages VII–XVI) provides a detailed explanation of how to use the activity sheets in the classroom and suggests various ways to construct the timeline using the completed activity sheets.

You can construct the timeline any way you see fit. Use the Timeline Components (pages XVIII–XXVI) to connect the activity sheets. Below are two possible timelines, constructed from the activity sheets in this unit and the Timeline Components.

Option 1: Basic Timeline

Construct this timeline to identify only the essential elements of the period.

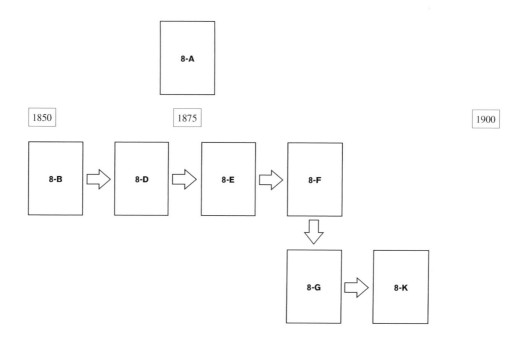

Option 2: Complete Timeline

Construct this timeline to identify the essential elements of the period, examine them in greater detail, and extend student learning.

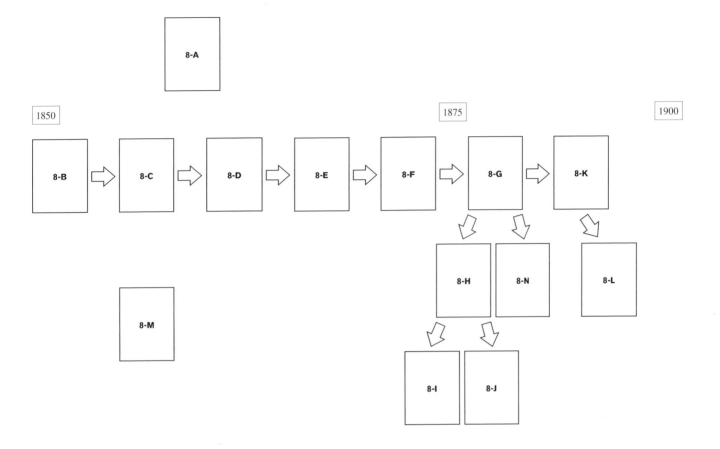

CRITICAL THINKING SKILLS

The activity sheets in this unit address various critical thinking skills. In addition, the constructed timeline emphasizes the essential critical thinking skills of identifying main ideas and details, sequencing events, and relating causes and effects.

Identifying Main Ideas and Details

Point out that Activity Sheet 8-A outlines the main ideas of the unit. Explain that the topics of the other activity sheets in the unit reflect the main ideas of the historical period the students are studying. Further explain that some activity sheets focus on the details related to specific topics.

As you and the students construct the timeline, show them that the following activity sheets form main idea/detail relationships: 8-G/8-H, 8-G/8-N, 8-H/8-I, 8-H/8-J, and 8-K/8-L. Have the students annotate the Timeline Arrows appropriately. Challenge the students to find similar relationships or create them by rearranging the activity sheets.

Sequencing Events

Point out that the activity sheets that make up the timeline are sequential. Show the students how the Timeline Dates provide a concrete reference for when events happened and how they relate to other events. (For example, the Compromise of 1850 happened before the Kansas-Nebraska Act was passed in 1854.) Make sure the students see that the Timeline Arrows indicate a chronological flow from left to right.

Relating Causes and Effects

As you and the students construct the timeline, show them that Activity Sheets 8-B through 8-E focus on the causes of the effects addressed on Activity Sheets 8-F and 8-G. Have the students annotate the Timeline Arrows appropriately. Challenge the students to find similar relationships or create them by rearranging the activity sheets.

INDIVIDUAL ACTIVITY SHEET NOTES

The notes below provide a variety of tips on how to guide the students through the completion and extension of each activity sheet.

8-A. The Civil War and Reconstruction

This activity sheet is most appropriate for the students to complete with partners, in small groups, or as a whole class. For example, you might want to complete the questions with the whole class at the beginning of the unit and then have the students answer the questions at the end of the unit. Encourage the students to think of additional questions related to the topic.

8-B. The Compromise of 1850

Explain that the Compromise of 1850 did decrease tensions in the United States but that it proved to be only the calm before the storm.

8-C. *Uncle Tom's Cabin*

You might want to read an excerpt from this novel, especially the exciting scene where the escapee Eliza is crossing the frozen Ohio River with her son. You might also share with the students the story that when Abraham Lincoln and Harriet Beecher Stowe were introduced, the President supposedly referred to her as, "the little lady who wrote the book that made this big war." Ask the students to explain his remark.

8-D. The Kansas-Nebraska Act

Point out that this act, which allowed slavery in a vast territory, was extremely divisive and it inflamed passions on both sides of the slavery debate.

8-E. Differences Between the North and the South

Make sure the students list differences besides views toward slavery, including differences in population, urbanization, and industrialization.

8-F. A Nation Divided

Consider having students annotate the map with the location of major battles of the war and their dates.

8-G. Major Events of the Civil War

Have the students list major battles and other significant events, such as the issuance of the Emancipation Proclamation. Encourage the students to write a brief description of each item's significance on the timeline.

8-H. Biography: Abraham Lincoln

Have the students read some of Lincoln's quotations. Then, have each student write his or her favorite quotation on the activity sheet. You might want to ask the students to create short biographical booklets about this quintessential American, using the activity sheet as a starting point.

8-I. A Voice From the Past: The Gettysburg Address

Ask the students why they think this speech is famous.

8-J. Lincoln's Assassination

Ask interested students to research and give reports about the fate of John Wilkes Booth's co-conspirators.

8-K. Reconstruction

Make sure the students understand the meaning of the word "reconstruction." Discuss the experiences of newly freed African Americans in the South.

8-L. Map Study: The United States in 1870

Have the students compare and contrast this map and the maps on Activity Sheets 5-P and 8-F. Emphasize the growing population and its increasing urbanization.

8-M. The Time Machine: Toys and Games

Help the students identify the main points of the essay, which should be written in the left-hand circle of the Venn diagram.

8-N. A Postcard From the Past: Gettysburg National Military Park

Suggest that the students visit www.nps.gov (the web site of the National Park Service) to gather information about Gettysburg National Military Park.

In the box below, draw a picture or attach a picture from a magazine or the Internet that represents this period of American history. The picture can be of anything you think is appropriate.

Ask questions about this period of American history. Then, answer them.

Question: WHO _____?

Answer: _____

Question: WHAT _____?

Answer: _____

Question: WHERE _____?

Answer: _____

Question: WHEN _____?

Answer: _____

Question: WHY _____?

Answer: _____

Question: HOW _____?

Answer: _____

This important date in American history is brought to you by

_____

Timeline markings (left): 1800, 1810, 1820, 1830, 1840, 1850, 1860, 1870, 1880, 1890, 1900

Timeline markings (right): 1900, 1890, 1880, 1870, 1860, 1850, 1840, 1830, 1820, 1810, 1800

1800

1810

1820

1830

1840

1850

1860

1870

1880

1890

1900

Complete the diagram below.

CAUSES

EFFECTS

The Compromise of 1850

What It Was: _____

_____

_____

_____

_____

_____

1900

1890

1880

1870

1860

1850

1840

1830

1820

1810

1800

This important date in American history is brought to you by

_____

Complete the diagram below. Draw an appropriate illustration on the book cover.

EFFECTS

DESCRIPTION

UNCLE TOM'S CABIN

YEAR PUBLISHED

WRITTEN BY: _____

1800
1810
1820
1830
1840
1850
1860
1870
1880
1890
1900

1900
1890
1880
1870
1860
1850
1840
1830
1820
1810
1800

This important date in American history is brought to you by

_____

★1854★ The Kansas-Nebraska Act

Complete the diagram below.

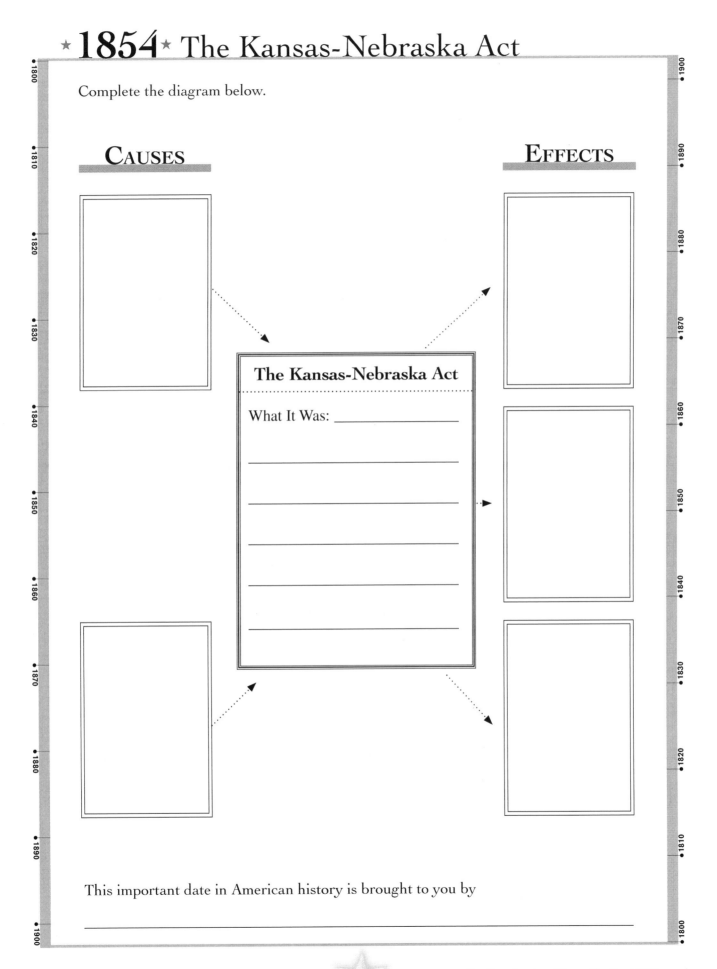

CAUSES

EFFECTS

The Kansas-Nebraska Act

What It Was: _____

_____

_____

_____

_____

_____

This important date in American history is brought to you by

_____

1800
1810
1820
1830
1840
1850
1860
1870
1880
1890
1900

★ 1860 ★ Differences Between the North and the South

Shade and label the North and South in 1860 on the map below. List facts about the North and facts about the South on the chart below. Then, list facts about things the two groups had in common.

North	South

Common Facts	

This important date in American history is brought to you by

_____

1900
1890
1880
1870
1860
1850
1840
1830
1820
1810
1800

★1861–1865★ A Nation Divided

Make a map key to identify the states of the Union, the territories of the Union, and the states of the Confederacy. Shade and label the following items on the map below: states of the Union, territories of the Union, and states of the Confederacy.

MAP KEY

☐ States of the Union

☐ Territories of the Union

☐ States of the Confederacy

This important date in American history is brought to you by

____

★ 1861–1865 ★ Major Events of the Civil War

Complete the timeline below.

_____ **1861**

A Confederate Soldier

_____ **1862**

_____ **1863**

A Union Soldier

_____ **1864**

_____ **1865**

This important date in American history is brought to you by

_____

Answer the questions below.

THE MAN

When did he live? _____

What do we know about his early life? _____

_____

_____

_____

What words would you use to describe him? _____

_____

_____

HIS CONTRIBUTIONS

What was the Emancipation Proclamation? _____

_____

_____

What is your favorite quotation by Abraham Lincoln? _____

_____

_____

How do we honor Abraham Lincoln today? _____

_____

This important date in American history is brought to you by

_____

The Gettysburg Address

Read Abraham Lincoln's speech below. Then, answer the questions.

"Four score and seven years ago our fathers brought forth on this continent a new nation, conceived in Liberty and dedicated to the proposition that all men are created equal. Now we are engaged in a great civil war, testing whether that nation or any nation so conceived and so dedicated can long endure. We are met on a great battlefield of that war. We have come to dedicate a portion of that field as a final resting place for those who here gave their lives that that nation might live. It is altogether fitting and proper that we should do this. But in a larger sense, we cannot dedicate, we cannot consecrate, we cannot hallow this ground. The brave men, living and dead who struggled here have consecrated it far above our poor power to add or detract. The world will little note nor long remember what we say here, but it can never forget what they did here. It is for us the living rather to be dedicated here to the unfinished work which they who fought here have thus far so nobly advanced. It is rather for us to be here dedicated to the great task remaining before us—that from these honored dead we take increased devotion to that cause for which they gave the last full measure of devotion—that we here highly resolve that these dead shall not have died in vain, that this nation under God shall have a new birth of freedom, and that government of the people, by the people, for the people shall not perish from the earth."

—Abraham Lincoln

What is Lincoln's main point? _____

_____

How does he describe the United States? _____

_____

What does Lincoln say the "test" of the war is? _____

_____

This important date in American history is brought to you by

_____

Study the illustration below. Then, write a caption for it that tells about what happened there on the night of April 14, 1865. Your caption should tell what happened, and who was involved.

FORD'S THEATRE IN WASHINGTON, D.C.

_____

_____

_____

_____

_____

This important date in American history is brought to you by

_____

Answer the questions below.

What was Reconstruction? _____

_____

What does this picture show about Reconsrtuction?_____

_____

Who were carpetbaggers and scalawags? _____

_____

Why were the Constitutional amendments passed after the Civil War important? _____

_____

This important date in American history is brought to you by

_____

Label the following items on the map below: U.S. states in 1870,
U.S. possessions in 1870, several major cities, and major bodies of water.

Fill in the missing information below. Record the total population, and shade the circle
graph to illustrate the rural/urban distribution.

THE UNITED STATES IN 1870

Total Population: _____

Rural/Urban Distribution:_____

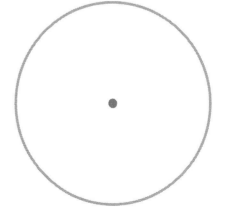

This important date in American history is brought to you by

_____

Activate the Time Machine to learn about toys and games during the middle 1800s. In the left-hand circle, write facts about toys and games during that time. In the right-hand circle, write facts about toys and games today. In the space where the circles overlap, write facts about toys and games that both time periods have in common.

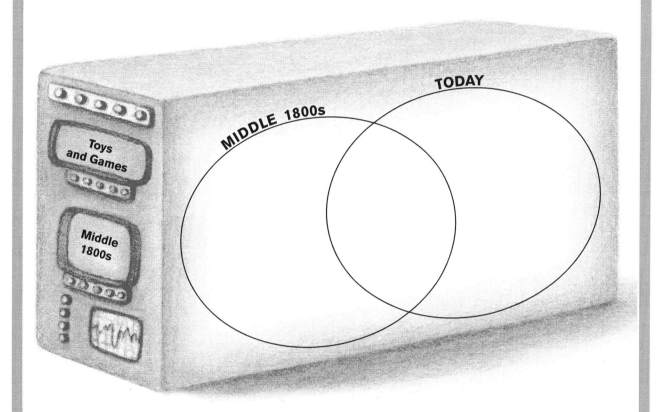

American children played with many different toys in the middle 1800s. Most of the toys were homemade. Dolls were very popular. They were made from leftover scraps of cloth and sometimes corn husks. Other popular toys included hoops, which were rolled along the ground with sticks, cup-and-ball toys, tops, and yo-yos.

Children made up a countless number of games to play, using their imagination and simple homemade toys like leather balls. Children often played outside. They ran races against each other and had pretend races with toy horses. A favorite pastime of smaller children was playing make-believe.

This important trip into American history is brought to you by

_____

★ Gettysburg National Military Park ★

The Battle of Gettysburg was a turning point in the Civil War. Today, the battlefield is preserved as Gettysburg National Military Park. What is it like to visit there? Conduct research to find out.

Use the Internet or any other resources your teacher suggests. Read the articles, and study the illustrations. When you have gathered enough information, make a postcard.

On the front of the postcard, draw a picture or attach a picture from a magazine or the Internet that gives some information about Gettysburg National Military Park. On the back of the postcard, write a caption that explains the picture. Then, write a note to a friend that tells about things to do and see at the park.

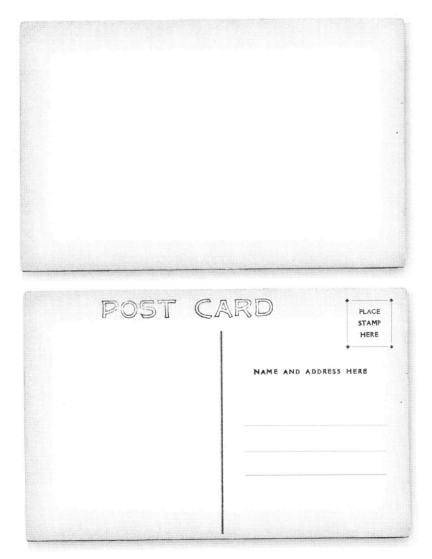

POST CARD

PLACE STAMP HERE

NAME AND ADDRESS HERE

This important place in American history is brought to you by

★ Unit 1 ★   Assessment

Discovery and Exploration: Prehistory–1606

A. Identifying Main Ideas and Details

Match each term on the left to its description on the right. Write the correct letter in the blank.

_____ 1. Beringia   **A.** explored North America for France

_____ 2. carrack   **B.** a rugged ship used by European explorers

_____ 3. Columbian Exchange   **C.** explored North America for England

_____ 4. John Cabot   **D.** the transfer of plants and animals between "old" and "new" worlds

_____ 5. Samuel de Champlain

                                       E. the land bridge between Asia and North America

B. Sequencing Events

Number the events below to show the order in which they happened. Write the correct number in each blank.

_____ Christopher Columbus discovers America.

_____ The first Americans cross Beringia.

_____ Europeans claim most of North America.

_____ Europeans seek a sea route to Asia.

_____ Culture areas develop in North America.

★ Unit 1 ★   Assessment

Discovery and Exploration: Prehistory–1606

C. Relating Causes and Effects

Write a paragraph that explains how the Europeans claimed North America for themselves.

_____

_____

_____

_____

_____

_____

D. Expressing an Opinion

Do you think Europeans had the right to claim North America? Explain your answer.

_____

_____

_____

_____

_____

_____

★ Unit 2 ★   Assessment

Colonial America: 1585–1776

A. Identifying Main Ideas and Details

Match each term on the left to its description on the right. Write the correct letter in the blank.

_____ 1. CROATOAN   **A.** the leader of Jamestown

_____ 2. compact   **B.** English colonies

_____ 3. John Smith   **C.** the Pilgrims' ship

_____ 4. Mayflower   **D.** a mysterious message at Roanoke Island

_____ 5. New England,   **E.** an agreement
          Middle, Southern

B. Sequencing Events

Number the events below to show the order in which they happened. Write the correct number in each blank.

_____ Jamestown is settled.

_____ The French and Indian War begins.

_____ The Pilgrims have the first Thanksgiving feast.

_____ The Quartering Act goes into effect.

_____ The colony at Roanoke Island is "lost."

★ Unit 2 ★

Assessment

Colonial America: 1585–1776

C. Relating Causes and Effects

Write a paragraph that explains why Plymouth was founded.

_____

_____

_____

_____

_____

_____

D. Expressing an Opinion

Do you think Jamestown would have survived without the help of Native Americans? Explain your answer.

_____

_____

_____

_____

_____

_____

NAME _____   DATE _____

★ Unit 3 ★   Assessment
The Revolutionary Period: 1765–1783

A. Identifying Main Ideas and Details

Match each term on the left to its description on the right. Write the correct letter in the blank.

_____ 1. Charles Townshend   **A.** where the Revolutionary War began

_____ 2. Intolerable Acts   **B.** issued the Declaration of Independence

_____ 3. Lexington and Concord   **C.** punishment for the Boston Tea Party

_____ 4. George Washington   **D.** the person in charge of British government revenue

_____ 5. Second Continental
          Congress   **E.** led American troops

B. Sequencing Events

Number the events below to show the order in which they happened. Write the correct number in each blank.

_____ The Revolutionary War begins.

_____ The Treaty of Paris is signed.

_____ The Intolerable Acts are passed.

_____ The Boston Massacre takes place.

_____ The Declaration of Independence is issued.

★ Unit 3 ★   Assessment
The Revolutionary Period: 1765–1783

C. Relating Causes and Effects

Write a paragraph that explains why the American colonies rebelled against the British government.

_____

_____

_____

_____

_____

_____

D. Expressing an Opinion

Do you think the British soldiers were justified in firing at the colonists during the Boston Massacre? Explain your answer.

_____

_____

_____

_____

_____

_____

★ Unit 4 ★   Assessment
Creating the Constitution: 1781–1803

A. Identifying Main Ideas and Details

Match each term on the left to its description on the right. Write the correct letter in the blank.

_____ 1. Preamble   **A.** failed to create a strong national government

_____ 2. Articles of Confederation   **B.** the first ten amendments to the Constitution

_____ 3. Bill of Rights   **C.** the "Father of the Constitution"

_____ 4. Federalism   **D.** a system in which state and
                                        national governments share power

_____ 5. James Madison

                                  E. the introduction to the Constitution

B. Sequencing Events

Number the events below to show the order in which they happened. Write the correct number in each blank.

_____ *Marbury* v. *Madison* is decided.

_____ The Federalists and the Anti-Federalists debate.

_____ The Articles of Confederation is written.

_____ The Constitutional Convention is held.

_____ Shays' Rebellion takes place.

★ Unit 4 ★   Assessment

Creating the Constitution: 1781–1803

C. Relating Causes and Effects

Write a paragraph that explains why the Constitutional Convention was held.

_____

_____

_____

_____

_____

_____

D. Expressing an Opinion

Do you think any rights should have been added or removed from the Bill of Rights? Explain your answer.

_____

_____

_____

_____

_____

★ Unit 5 ★   Assessment

Expanding the Country: 1790–1860

A. Identifying Main Ideas and Details

Match each term on the left to its description on the right. Write the correct letter in the blank.

_____ 1. Manifest Destiny   A. the belief that the United States should
                                                expand throughout all of North America

_____ 2. Mexican Cession
                                            B. used heavily by traders

_____ 3. Lewis and Clark
            expedition   C. a popular destination in 1849

_____ 4. California   D. result of the Mexican War in 1846–1848

_____ 5. Santa Fe Trail   E. explored the Louisiana Purchase

B. Sequencing Events

Number the events below to show the order in which they happened. Write the correct number in each blank

_____ Louisiana Purchase

_____ California Gold Rush

_____ "Great Migration" on the Oregon Trail

_____ Texas Annexation

_____ Gadsden Purchase

⋆ Unit 5 ⋆   Assessment

Expanding the Country: 1790–1860

C. Relating Causes and Effects

Write a paragraph that explains some of the results of Americans' belief in Manifest Destiny.

_____

_____

_____

_____

_____

D. Expressing an Opinion

Would you like to have accompanied Lewis and Clark on their expedition? Explain your answer.

_____

_____

_____

_____

_____

★ Unit 6 ★   Assessment

An Age of Advancements: 1790–1860

A. Identifying Main Ideas and Details

Match each term on the left to its description on the right. Write the correct letter in the blank.

_____ 1. telegraph   **A.** developed interchangeable parts

_____ 2. Eli Whitney   **B.** invented a plow

_____ 3. Lowell   **C.** the "lightning line"

_____ 4. *Clermont*   **D.** a successful steamboat

_____ 5. John Deere   **E.** the birthplace of the American
                                      Industrial Revolution

B. Sequencing Events

Number the events below to show the order in which they happened. Write the correct number in each blank

_____ The telegraph is invented.

_____ The Erie Canal is completed.

_____ The cotton gin is invented.

_____ Lowell, Massachusetts, is founded.

_____ The mechanical reaper is invented.

★ Unit 6 ★   Assessment

An Age of Advancements: 1790–1860

C. Relating Causes and Effects

Write a paragraph that explains how the growth of the railroad system affected the United States.

_____

_____

_____

_____

_____

_____

D. Expressing an Opinion

What do you think the most important invention during the first half of the 1800s was? Explain your answer.

_____

_____

_____

_____

_____

_____

★ Unit 7 ★   Assessment

Social Issues: 1790–1860

A. Identifying Main Ideas and Details

Match each term on the left to its description on the right. Write the correct letter in the blank.

_____ 1. Seneca Falls   **A.** fought to keep their freedom

_____ 2. abolitionists   **B.** disaster for Native Americans

_____ 3. Underground Railroad   **C.** people opposed to slavery

_____ 4. Trail of Tears   **D.** a way for slaves to escape to freedom

_____ 5. Seminoles   **E.** location of the first women's
                                                 rights convention

B. Sequencing Events

Number the events below to show the order in which they happened. Write the correct number in each blank

_____ Indian Removal Act

_____ Missouri Compromise

_____ Seminole War

_____ Seneca Falls Convention

_____ Trail of Tears

⋆ Unit 7 ⋆   Assessment

Social Issues: 1790–1860

C. Relating Causes and Effects

Write a paragraph that explains the effects of the Indian Removal Act on Native Americans.

_____

_____

_____

_____

_____

_____

D. Expressing an Opinion

Think about the people you researched in this unit. Which one do you admire most? Explain your answer

_____

_____

_____

_____

_____

_____

★ Unit 8 ★   Assessment

The Civil War and Reconstruction: 1850–1877

A. Identifying Main Ideas and Details

Match each term on the left to its description on the right. Write the correct letter in the blank.

_____ 1. Harriet Beecher Stowe   **A.** assassinated Lincoln

_____ 2. Reconstruction   **B.** location of a key battle of the Civil War

_____ 3. Gettysburg   **C.** the author of *Uncle Tom's Cabin*

_____ 4. Kansas-Nebraska Act   **D.** reunited the country

_____ 5. John Wilkes Booth   **E.** increased division between the North
                                              and the South

B. Sequencing Events

Number the events below to show the order in which they happened. Write the correct number in each blank.

_____ Reconstruction begins.

_____ The Civil War begins.

_____ The Kansas-Nebraska Act is passed.

_____ The Compromise of 1850 is passed.

_____ *Uncle Tom's Cabin* is published.

★ Unit 8 ★

Assessment

The Civil War and Reconstruction: 1850–1877

C. Relating Causes and Effects

Write a paragraph that explains the causes of the Civil War.

_____

_____

_____

_____

_____

_____

D. Expressing an Opinion

Why do you think so many Americans visit Civil War battlefields?

_____

_____

_____

_____

_____

_____

1-A. Discovery and Exploration

Questions will vary, but should be relevant to the unit. Ensure answers are correct.

1-B. Map Study: North America

Maps will vary but should identify the major physical features of North America.

1-C. The First Americans

Maps will vary but should be labeled properly and indicate an understanding of Beringia's general location and that it was a land bridge.

1-D. Native American Culture Areas

Maps will vary depending on the source used, but should accurately reflect the source and include appropriate labels and symbols.

1-E. Trade with Asia

WHY: They wanted to trade to obtain valued goods and to make money. They wanted to find a sea route to circumvent the Muslims who controlled the overland routes.

WHAT: Many goods were traded, among them silk and spices. The first sea route was east, around the tip of Africa.

WHO: Prince Henry the Navigator sponsored many trips. Vasco da Gama reached India.

WHEN: Trade began in the by 100 BC, but it was at its peak in the 1300s and 1400s. Sea trade began in the late 1400s and early 1500s.

HOW: Columbus hoped to shorten the route by sailing west instead of east. Columbus was searching for a trade route when he reached North America.

1-F. The Explorers' Ship

The lateen sail enabled the ship to sail into the wind. The rectangular sails were used to sail with the wind. A large hold was needed on long voyages to carry supplies. The smooth sides decreased water resistance. The large rudder enabled swift and sure turns. The forecastle and sterncastle were used as shelter for the sailors.

1-G. Biography: Christopher Columbus

Columbus lived from 1451 to 1506. He was Italian. Descriptive words will vary: brave, daring, etc. Columbus sailed for Spain. His three ships were the Nina, the Pinta, and the Santa Maria. His purpose was to sail west to Asia. He discovered America for the Europeans of the time. He was not looking for America when he happened upon it. Columbus thought he was in the Indies and so named the inhabitants "Indians."

1-H. The Columbian Exchange

The Columbian Exchange is the movement of individuals, peoples, cultures, ideas, tools, goods, plants, animals, diseases, and other things between the Americas and Europe.

From the Americas to Europe

Plants: cacao, maize (corn), peanut, potato, rubber tree, sweet potato, tobacco, tomato
Animals: gray squirrel, guinea pig, llama, muskrat, turkey

Other: people, ideas

From Europe to the Americas

Plants: barley, citrus fruits, coffee, peas, sugar, wheat

Animals: cat, cattle, chicken, goat, honeybee, horse, pig, sheep

Other: diseases (measles, smallpox, influenza)

1-I. A Voice from the Past: Christopher Columbus

He did not think of them as equals; he thought of them as potential servants. The condescension and racism became the typical European view. Answers will vary, but should be explained. Point out the ironic conclusion to the complimentary assessment.

1-J. Exploring North America

Answers may vary slightly.

John Cabot: England; 1497-1498; NE North America

Amerigo Vespucci: Italy, Portugal; 1499-1504; South America

Vasco Núñez de Balboa: Spain; 1513; Central America

Juan Ponce de León: Spain; 1513; SE North America

Giovanni da Verrazano: Italy; 1524; NE North America

Sebastian Cabot: England; 1526-1530; NE North America

Jacques Cartier: France; 1535; NE North America

Hernando de Soto: Spain; 1539-1542; SE North America

Francisco de Coronado: Spain; 1540-1542; SW North America

Martin Frobisher: England; 1576-1578; NE North America

Juan de Oñate: Spain; 1598-1605; SW North America

Samuel de Champlain: France; 1603-1613; NE North America

1-K. Cabot Explores North America for England

Check maps for accuracy. Paragraphs will vary, but should indicate that the Italian Cabot, sailing for England, reached northern North America in 1497 while looking for a sea route to Asia.

1-L. Coronado Explores North America for Spain

Check maps for accuracy. Paragraphs will vary, but should indicate that Coronado explored the American southwest in search of the legendary Seven Cities of Cíbola.

1-M. Champlain Explores North America for France

Check maps for accuracy. Paragraphs will vary, but should indicate that Champlain founded Quebec and explored the region around it for many years.

1-N. European Claims in North America

Maps will vary slightly depending on the source used, but should accurately reflect the source and include accurate labels.

1-0. The Time Machine: Transportation

Answers will vary. Generally:

Before Europeans Arrived: most travel on foot, much use of boats, snow travel methods

Today: examples of mechanized transport

Both: transportation important, some of the same methods used

1-P. A Postcard from the Past: Native Americans in Your Community

Reward research and earnest attempts.

Unit 2

2-A. Colonial America

Questions will vary, but should be relevant to the unit. Ensure answers are correct.

2-B. The Lost Colony

It was located on Roanoke Island in Virginia. It was established by England. There were 117 colonists (118 with the birth of Virginia Dare). Their leader was John White. Virginia Dare was the first English child born in America. "CROATOAN" was found carved on a post when White belatedly returned from England with supplies. Their fate is unclear; some likely died or were killed, others may have mingled with various American Indians.

2-C. Jamestown

permanent; Virginia; gold; tobacco

2-D. Biography: John Smith and Pocahontas

Smith lived from c. 1580 to 1631. He was English. He helped the colonists as their leader by enforcing rules, making people work, and negotiating with local Indians. Descriptive words will vary. Samples: strong, brave, smart, etc. Pocahontas lived from c. 1595 to 1617. She was of Powhatan's tribe. She helped settlers by, supposedly, saving Smith's life and working to maintain good relations between them and her father, the chief. Descriptive words will vary. Samples: brave, clever, smart, etc. Smith and Pocahontas cooperated to help Jamestown settlers survive.

2-E. The Pilgrims

The Pilgrims were English Separatists. Their leaders were John Carver and William Bradford. They sailed to America because, living in Holland meant not being able to own land and having their children influenced by a different culture. Their ship was the Mayflower. Their settlement was Plymouth Colony. Native Americans helped the Pilgrims fish and grow food and left them in peace.

2-F. A Voice from the Past: The Mayflower Compact

Answers will vary. The excerpt means that the Pilgrims agreed to make just laws and abide by them. They needed laws to avoid division and to maintain order.

2-G. The First Thanksgiving

Answers will vary. The feast was held as a celebration of harvest and as a social gathering. They likely felt thankful for survival in a difficult environment. The picture indicates that the Pilgrims cooperated with American Indians, maintained European customs, and were religious. Most Americans view Thanksgiving as a time to identify the things they are thankful for.

2-H. Map Study: Colonial America

Maps may vary slightly depending on the source used, but should accurately reflect the source and be labeled accurately.

2-I. The New England Colonies

Answers may vary slightly.

Massachusetts; 1620; religious freedom; fishing, lumber, sea trade

New Hampshire; 1623; fishing and trade post; fishing and trade

Connecticut; 1636; Puritan settlement; sea trade

Rhode Island; 1636; religious freedom from intolerance in Massachusetts; shipping; farming

The Pilgrims established Massachusetts. Rhode Island was established by people from Massachusetts. Ships were important for fishing and trade.

2-J. The Middle Colonies

Answers may vary slightly.

New York; 1625; expansion; farming, lumber, shipbuilding trade

Delaware; 1638; trading post; trade, farming

New Jersey; 1664; trading post; religious freedom; trade, farming

Pennsylvania; 1637; to establish a Quaker settlement; religious tolerance; trade, farming

The Quakers established Pennsylvania. Farming and trade were the two main economic activities.

2-K. The Southern Colonies

Virginia; 1607; search for gold; tobacco farming

Maryland; 1632; freedom of worship for Catholics; tobacco farming

North Carolina; 1663; English expansion; tobacco and indigo farming

South Carolina; 1663; English expansion; tobacco and indigo farming

Georgia; 1732; debtor settlement; rice and indigo farming; lumber; trade

Virginia was the site of Jamestown. Tobacco was an important crop. Maryland was established for religious reasons.

2-L. The French and Indian War

The war was fought between the French and their Indian allies and England. England won the war. The main effect of the war was the transfer of vast amounts of French territory in North America to the English, and the English consolidation of power in North America.

2-M. The Quartering Act

Sentences will vary, but should indicate the colonists' opposition to the act, viewed as overbearing and intrusive, and the soldiers' support of the act as necessary and proper.

2-N. The Time Machine: Education

Answers will vary. Generally:

Colonial Period: poor children educated at home, relatives for teachers, non-academic subjects, different things taught boys and girls, schools in homes, Biblical lessons, use of hornbooks.

Today: widespread public education, greater variety, emphasis on academics, etc.

Both: learning of "the basics," taught by adults, going to school, memorization

2-0. A Postcard from the Past: Colonial Williamsburg

Reward research and earnest attempts.

3-A. The Revolutionary Period

Questions will vary, but should be relevant to the unit. Ensure answers are correct.

3-B. "No Taxation without Representation"

Answers may vary slightly.

Causes of the acts included the British desire to increase revenue from the colonies (Britain had spent a great deal during the French and Indian War) and the British desire to tighten control over its colonies. Effects of the Sugar Act include protests by American rum producers (they used molasses to make rum) and the eventual lowering of the tax. Effects of the Stamp Act include riots and boycotts and an organized, unified protest called the Stamp Act Congress.

3-C. The Townshend Acts

Townshend was the British Chancellor of the Exchequer. The Townshend Acts were passed to punish the colonists and to raise revenue. The Townshend Acts placed duties on imported goods and set up an agency to collect the duties. The goods were paper, paint, glass, lead, and tea. The colonists protested the Townshend Acts and boycotted goods. The Townshend Acts were repealed, except for the one that affected tea.

3-D. The Boston Massacre

Sentences will vary, but should indicate the colonists' opposition to the Townshend Acts and the soldiers' fear of the mob.

3-E. The Boston Tea Party

Captions will vary but should indicate that the Boston Tea Party was a protest against the Tea Act, and that the protestors were led by Samuel Adams.

3-F. The Intolerable Acts

Boston Port Bill; to punish colonists for their defiance; closed Boston Harbor until tea destroyed in Boston Tea Party paid for

Massachusetts Government Act; to punish colonists for their defiance; set up military government and limited colonists' meetings

Administration of Justice Act; to punish colonists for their defiance; enabled British officials to be tried in England

Quartering Act; to punish colonists for their defiance; required colonists to house British troops

Main Effect: the calling of the First Continental Congress

The Intolerable Acts were so-called by the colonists because the thought they were harsh and unbearable.

3-G. The First Continental Congress

Answers will vary.

We are meeting because we want to protest recent British actions, especially the Intolerable Acts.

We want to tell King George III that we want a bigger say in how we are governed.

Some of our leaders are George Washington, Patrick Henry, and Samuel Adams.

We have set up the Continental Association to halt the import and use of British goods.

We will meet again if British policy toward us does not change.

3-H. The War Begins

Answers will vary but should indicate that the British marched toward Concord to destroy an American arms stockpile and engaged (or were engaged by Minutemen) along the way, at Lexington. When they reached Concord, they again fought.

3-I. A Voice From the Past: The Declaration of Independence

That all men are created equal, that they are endowed by their Creator with certain unalienable Rights, that among these are Life, Liberty and the pursuit of Happiness.

The purpose of government is to secure the unalienable rights of men.

3-J. Battles of the Revolutionary War

Maps will vary depending on the source used, but should accurately reflect the source and include appropriate labels and symbols in the key. Major Battles included the battles of Lexington, Concord, Saratoga, Breed's Hill, Princeton, Trenton, and Yorktown.

3-K. Biography: George Washington

George Washington lived from 1792 to 1799.

He is called the "Father of Our Country" because he was the leader during the Revolutionary War. He also presided over the Constitutional convention, and he was the country's first President.

He commanded the Continental Army, leading it to victory over the British.

His home was Mount Vernon.

"First in war" as the commander of the Continental Army, "first in peace" as a national leader, presiding over the Constitutional Convention and becoming the first President, and "first in the hearts of his countrymen" as a beloved figure.

3-L. The Treaty of Paris

Answers may vary slightly. Major provisions included:

Great Britain recognized the United States as independent.

Great Britain would withdraw its remaining troops.

The United States' northern border with British Canada was set.

The United States' western border with Spanish territory was set as the Mississippi River.

The United States southern border with Spanish Florida was set.

The United States would have fishing rights off the coast of Nova Scotia.

The United States would not persecute any Americans that had remained loyal to Great Britain.

3-M. Map Study: The United States in 1783

Maps will vary depending on the source used, but should accurately reflect the source and include appropriate labels. The demographic data should be graphed correctly.

3-N. The Time Machine: Food

Answers will vary. Generally:

Colonial Period: people provided food for themselves, hunting an important source of food, bread made at home, meat and bread for breakfast

Today: widespread availability of prepared foods purchased

Both: eating meat, bread, stew

3-0. A Postcard from the Past: Independence National Historic Park

Reward research and earnest attempts.

4-A. Creating the Constitution

Questions will vary, but should be relevant to the unit. Ensure answers are correct.

4-B. The Articles of Confederation

Who Created: The Continental Congress

Why Created: for a plan of government for the new country

Main Weaknesses: weak national government, no chief executive, no power to tax or help states

4-C. Shays' Rebellion

Answers may vary slightly.

Causes include: states increasing taxes to repay debts; debt-ridden farmers; sale of farm property to pay tax; debtors prisons

Effects include: demonstration of citizens' willingness to defy government; demonstration of the weaknesses of the Articles of Confederation; the calling of the Constitutional Convention

4-D. The Constitutional Convention

Captions will vary, but should indicate that the Constitutional Convention was held to develop a new plan of government, that it was held in Independence Hall in Philadelphia, and that the result was the Constitution.

4-E. Biography: James Madison and Benjamin Franklin

Answers may vary slightly:

Madison: Lived 1751 to 1836. Major accomplishments include serving in the Continental Congress, working at the Constitutional Convention, serving in the House of Representatives, serving as Secretary of State, and serving as President. Called "Father of the Constitution" because of the leading role he played in shaping the document at the Constitutional Convention and championing the Constitution's ratification.

Franklin: Lived 1706-1790. Major accomplishments: many and varied, including publisher, scientists, organizer of a hospital, university, and library, inventor of lightning rod, stove, and bifocals, ambassador, helping draft the Declaration of Independence.

4-F. The Federalists and the Anti-Federalists

Answers will vary. Federalist arguments focused on the usefulness of a strong central government

Anti-Federalist arguments focused on that strong central government would detract from states' and individuals' rights.

The Federalist was a collection of essays supporting the Constitution that originally appeared in newspapers.

4-G. The Constitution

Answers may vary slightly. Essentially:

Article I: the Legislative Branch

Article II: the Executive Branch

Article III: the Judicial Branch

Article IV: Relationships Among the States

Article V: Amendment Process

Article VI: General Provisions

Article VII: Ratification

4-H. A Voice From the Past: The Preamble to the Constitution

Beginning the Preamble with "We the People" emphasizes the primacy of citizens in creating and controlling the government. Reasons are (1) "to form a more perfect Union"; (2) "establish justice"; (3) "insure domestic tranquility"; (4) "provide for the common defense"; (5) "promote the general welfare," and; (6) "secure the blessings of liberty to ourselves and our posterity."

Answers will vary but should express the idea that general welfare means the well-being of all the people in the United States.

4-I. Federalism

Answers may vary slightly.

Delegated Powers: to regulate trade, issue money, conduct foreign relations, establish a postal system, raise armed forces, declare war, govern territories, regulate immigration, make "necessary and proper" laws

Concurrent Powers: to tax, borrow, establish courts, enforce laws, provide for citizens' welfare

Reserved powers: to regulate trade within the state, establish local governments, conduct elections, regulate voting, establish schools, incorporate businesses, issue licenses, keep powers not delegated or prohibited to states

Federalism: the sharing of power between the federal and state governments

4-J. Separation of Powers

Legislative Branch: to make laws

Executive Branch: to enforce laws

Judicial Branch: to interpret laws

Separation of Powers: three-way division of powers among the branches of government.

4-K. Checks and Balances

Answers may vary. Generally:

Legislative Checks Executive: can override vetoes; can impeach President; ratifies treaties, declares war, appropriates money

Legislative Checks Judicial: creates courts; can impeach judges; appoints judges; can pass new laws to override a finding of unconstitutionality

Executive Checks Legislative: can propose laws; can veto laws; can call special sessions; appoints officials

Executive Checks Judicial: appoints judges; can pardon offenders

Judicial Checks Legislative: can declare laws unconstitutional

Judicial Checks Executive: can declare executive acts unconstitutional

4-L. The Bill of Rights

Answers may vary slightly. Essentially:

First: freedoms of religion, speech, the press, assembly, and petition

Second: right to bear arms

Third: no quartering

Fourth: protection from unreasonable search and seizure

Fifth: protections of accused; no self-incrimination or double jeopardy; due process; right to own private property

Sixth: right to trial by jury and counsel

Seventh: trial by jury in certain kinds of cases

Eighth: no excessive bail or cruel and unusual punishment

Ninth: rights other than those listed are reserved for the people

Tenth: powers not delegated or prohibited are reserved to the states

4-M. *Marbury* v. *Madison*

Answers will vary. In 1803, William Marbury had been promised an appointment as a government official. Marbury claimed that under a law, the Judiciary Act of 1789, the Supreme Court could order Secretary of State James Madison to give Marbury the promised appointment. In its decision, the Court held that the Judiciary Act was unconstitutional. In doing so, it established the principle of judicial review.

Marbury v. Madison established the principle of judicial review.

Judicial Review: the Supreme Court's power to declare laws or presidential actions unconstitutional.

4-N. The Time Machine: Housing

Answers will vary. Generally:

Late 1700s: most people live on farms and in farmhouses; servants and slaves

Today: most people live in cities, wider variety of housing in style (like apartments) and building materials; such things as electricity, plumbing, and telephone service; live-in servants rare, no slavery

Both: housing important; many houses built of wood

4-0. A Postcard from the Past: The National Archives

Reward research and earnest attempts.

5-A. Expanding the Country

Questions will vary, but should be relevant to the unit. Ensure answers are correct.

5-B. Map Study: The United States in 1790

Maps will vary; check for essential accuracy. Population data: 3.9 million; 95% rural, 5% urban.

5-C. The Louisiana Purchase

Area of territory: 827,192 square miles

Acquired from: France

How it Was Acquired: purchased

Current States in Territory: all or part of Arkansas, Colorado, Iowa, Kansas, Louisiana, Minnesota, Missouri, Montana, Nebraska, New Mexico, North Dakota, Oklahoma, South Dakota, Texas, Wyoming

5-D. Lewis and Clark

Captions will vary, but should at least indicate that the expedition was sent to explore and investigate the territory acquired in the Louisiana Purchase and traveled up the Missouri River and westward to the Pacific.

5-E. Biography: Sacagewea

Sacagewea lived from about 1787 to 1812. She was Shoshone. Her name means "Bird Woman." She was married to the French-Canadian Touissant Charbonneau. Her brother was a Shoshone leader. She had two children. Descriptive words will vary: brave, caring, strong, etc. She served as interpreter, guide, and gathered food and medicine. Sacagewea is honored on a coin, in museums, and house geographical features are named for her.

5-F. The Florida Cessions

Area of territory: 58,560

Acquired from: Spain

How it Was Acquired: treaty agreement/purchase

Current States in Territory: all of Florida and parts of Alabama, Mississippi, and Florida

5-G. Manifest Destiny

Manifest Idea was that the United States' destiny was to cover and control North America

Examples include territorial acquisitions, westward migration, and Indian removal.

It affected Americans in a generally positive way as the country grew larger and more prosperous.

It affected Native Americans in a negative way as they were removed from their lands and mistreated.

Rewriting will vary, but should reflect the original sentence.

5-H. The Oregon Trail

Length: about 2,000 miles

Number of Settlers: 350,000 (1843-1869)

Average Time: 4 1/2 months

Percentage Survived: 90

Years Used: primarily 1843 (large-scale migration began)-1869 (transcontinental railroad opened)

5-I. The Texas Annexation

Area of territory: 390,143 square miles

Acquired from: Republic of Texas

How it Was Acquired: annexation

Current States in Territory: All Texas and parts of New Mexico, Oklahoma, Kansas, Colorado, and Wyoming

5-J. The Oregon Country Cession

Area of territory: 285,580 square miles

Acquired from: Great Britain

How it Was Acquired: treaty agreement

Current States in Territory: All of Oregon, Washington and Idaho and parts of Montana and Wyoming

5-K. The Mexican Cession

Area of territory: 529,017 square miles

Acquired from: Mexico

How it Was Acquired: treaty after Mexican War

Current States in Territory: All of California, Nevada, and Utah and parts of Wyoming, Colorado, Arizona, and New Mexico

5-L. The California Gold Rush

Answers may vary. The basic cause was the discovery of gold in California, augmented by President Polk's confirmation of it and his declaration that the gold was abundant. Major effects included the growth of San Francisco and other downs, the migration of hundreds of thousands of people to California, some miners growing rich, the displacement of Native Americans and Mexicans in California, and extensive environmental damage from hydraulic mining.

5-M. A Voice from the Past: San Francisco During the Gold Rush

Adjectives will vary. Samples: busy, dirty, exciting, noisy, confusing, etc. Whether students would like to have visited will vary, but should be explained.

5-N. The Santa Fe Trail

Began: Independence, Missouri

Ended: Santa Fe, New Mexico

Length: 900 miles

Years: 1821-1880

Why important to traders: Answers will vary, but should indicate that it was primarily a commercial highway.

5-0. The Gadsden Purchase

Area of territory: 29,640

Acquired from: Mexico

How it Was Acquired: purchase

Current States in Territory: Parts of Arizona and New Mexico

5-P. Map Study: The United States in 1860

Maps will vary; check for essential accuracy. Population data: 31.4 million; 80% rural, 20% urban

5-Q. The Time Machine: Entertainment

Answers will vary. Generally:

First Half of the 1800s: little time for entertainment; at home; visiting, games, toys, reading; out: dances, socials, fairs, church

Today: more leisure time; all of the 19th-century activities plus modern entertainments

Both: all of the 19th-century activities

5-R. A Postcard from the Past: Santa Fe National Historic Trail

Reward research and earnest attempts.

6-A. An Age of Advancements

Questions will vary, but should be relevant to the unit. Ensure answers are correct.

6-B. Biography: Eli Whitney

Answers may vary slightly. Eli Whitney lived from 1765 to 1825. He showed mechanical talent as a boy, making a violin at 12 and starting a nail-making business in his teens. He studied to be a teacher and a lawyer. Descriptive words might include talented, inventive, smart, etc. The interchangeable system uses standardized parts made by machine to facilitate mass production. Whitney made muskets. Interchangeable parts are necessary for mass production because they speed part-making and assembly.

6-C. The Steam Engine

Answers may vary slightly. Important to industrialization because it powered factory machines. Important to transportation because it powered locomotives and ships. Evans created the first successful high pressure steam engine and built the first steam-powered land vehicle in the United States.

6-D. Lowell and the Industrial Revolution

The Industrial Revolution was essentially the transformation from an agricultural society with home-based production of goods to an industrial society marked by mechanization. It occurred in the 1820s. Most industry was located in the northeastern United States. It changed life in many ways, including the growth of cities, the increase in numbers of employees, the availability of products, and so on. It is important because it dramatically changed life and ushered in styles of living that are still with us today.

6-E. A Voice from the Past: Life in a Factory Town

Descriptive words will vary. Samples: busy, hard, tiring etc. Assessment of treatment might vary but should be supported. Generally quite unfair.

6-F. American Industry in 1860

Answers will vary. It was different in that it was much more widespread and technologically advanced and more goods were mass produced. Most industry was located in the northeast. Industrialization gave workers jobs but they were often mistreated. Industry was key to the American economic boom of the period.

6-G. Eli Whitney's Cotton Gin

The cotton gin separated the seeds from cotton fibers. It led to increased production of cotton in the south. Increased production led to a greater demand for slaves.

6-H. Cyrus McCormick's Mechanical Reaper

It harvested grain and made agriculture more efficient. It enabled farmers to farm vast areas of the plains. It decreased the number of farm workers needed.

6-I. John Deere's Plow

Handles: two extensions at left (held by plow operator)

Moldboard: A curved metal plate at bottom (turned over earth)

Share: metal blade on mold board (cut into earth)

Beam: the wooden spine of the plow (other parts attach to it)

Hitch: fixture at right tip of beam (used to attach to horses)

Deere's plow was the first successful self-cleaning plow. It was needed to cut through the tough sod and operate in the denser soil. It contributed to expansion by making it feasible to mine the western plains.

6-J. American Agriculture in 1860

Answers will vary. It was different in that it was much more widespread, technologically advanced, and productive. Major crops included corn, wheat, rice, cotton, and tobacco. Most farms were located in the south and west.

6-K. The *Clermont*

Captions will vary but should indicate that the *Clermont* was the first commercially successful steamboat; it ran on the Hudson River in New York, it was built by Robert Fulton, and it was important because it ushered in a new era of steam-powered ships.

6-L. The National Road

Answers will vary. Facts: it was the country's first federal highway; construction began in 1811; went from Cumberland, Maryland and reached Vandalia, Illinois (by 1841); also known as the Cumberland Road; about 800 miles long; built to facilitate westward expansion. Important effects of road construction included an improved economy, greater availability of goods, increased travel, and speedier travel.

6-M. The Erie Canal

Check map for accuracy. Answers may vary slightly. The Erie Canal was built to connect the Atlantic seaboard to the Great Lakes region—east and west at the time—with a waterway to carry people, raw materials, and goods. It connected the Hudson River with Lake Erie, The original canal was 363 miles long. People traveled by horse-and ox-pulled flatboats. The Erie Canal was important because it provided a way west, to a regional economic boom, and inspired the construction of other canals.

6-N. The Railroads

Answers will vary, but should indicate the railroad construction accelerated, reflecting the importance and value of the railroad. The growth of the railroad system helped the economy, made travel much speedier, linked distant cities, and helped American expansion.

6-O. The Telegraph

Answers may vary slightly.

What: a machine to send information long distance

How: electronic signals sent over wire in a code of dots and dashes

Effects: nearly instantaneous transmission of news, long-distance coordination of news, messages, train schedules, military maneuvers, etc.

Who: Samuel F.B. Morse

6-P. American Transportation and Communication

Answers will vary. Generally: Major difference in transportation is advance of mechanized transport in the form of the steamboat and railway. Major methods included foot, horse, wagon, sailing ship, steamships, and railroad. Effects of improved transportation included economic boom and greater and speedier travel. Major difference in communication was advent of telegraph and improved postal service. Major methods included telegraph, mail, and other print sources (newspapers, magazines, and books). Effects of improved communication included economic, more communication, long-distance coordination of government and business activities, and "shrinking" of the nation.

6-Q. The Time Machine: Communication

Answers will vary. Generally:

First Half of the 1800s: slow mail, no envelopes, telegraph common, newspapers, magazines, books

Today: faster mail, overnight service, envelopes, telephone, fax, e-mail, Internet, etc.

Both: mail, newspapers, magazines, books

6-R. A Postcard from the Past: Lowell National Historical Park

Reward research and earnest attempts.

Unit 7

7-A. Social Issues

Questions will vary, but should be relevant to the unit. Ensure answers are correct.

7-B. Expansion and Native Americans

Answers will vary. The Bureau of Indian affairs was created to oversee Indian removal and minimize conflict with settlers. Facts will vary, but should indicate the negative effect of westward expansion on Native Americans.

7-C. The Indian Removal Act

Answers will vary. The Indian Removal Act authorized the relocation of several Indian nations from the east to Indian territory west of the Mississippi River. Descriptions will vary, but should indicate that the settlers' had a positive view of the act, which opened up new land for them, while the Native Americans had a negative view of it, which forced them from their homelands and caused great suffering.

7-D. The Trail of Tears

Captions will vary but should indicate that the Trail of Tears was the forced journeys of several Native American nations from their homelands in the east to the Indian Territory in the west, that it happened under the auspices of the Indian Removal Act, and that it is so-called because of the terrific hardships of the journeys.

7-E. The Seminole War

Answers will vary. The Seminole War was caused by Seminole resistance to their removal from Florida. It was fought between Seminole fighters and the U.S. Army. It ended with most Seminoles being forced to move, but many remaining in Florida.

7-F. Women's Rights

Answers will vary. The convention was held to call for equal social and civil rights for women, notably the right to vote. Facts will vary, but should indicate the second-class status of women during this time period.

7-G. The Seneca Falls Convention

Where: Seneca Falls, New York

Why: to call for equal rights for women

Who: Elizabeth Cady Stanton, Lucretia Mott, Frederick Douglass

How: the first such convention in history

What: document modeled on the Declaration of Independence calling for women's rights and stating "all men and women are created equal"

7-H. Biography: Elizabeth Cady Stanton and Frederick Douglass

Answers will vary. Stanton lived from 1815 to 1902. Her contributions included organizing the Seneca Falls Convention, wrote the Declaration of Sentiments, helped found the National Woman Suffrage Association, and persuaded a senator to sponsor what would become the 19th Amendment to the Constitution. Descriptive words will vary: smart, ahead of her time, brave, etc. Douglass lived from about 1818 to 1895. He spoke out against slavery, protested against segregation, worked on the Underground Railroad, and founded an abolitionist newspaper. Descriptive words will vary: courageous, intelligent, well-spoken, etc. Stanton and Douglass both worked to have all Americans treated equally.

7-I. A Voice from the Past: Sojourner Truth

Answers will vary. Truth's main point is that women are as strong as men and so should have equal rights. Her speech is compelling.

7-J. Slavery in the United States

Answers will vary. The ban did not end slavery because slavery itself was not affected by the ban on trade and because illicit trade continued. Facts will vary, but should reflect the abhorrent nature of the institution of slavery.

7-K. The Missouri Compromise

Answers will vary. Major causes of the Missouri compromise include the previously equal number of free and slave states before Missouri's admission to the union; the existence of slavery in Missouri, Missouri's petitioning to join the union, and Missouri's geographic location both north ad south of the Ohio River. Major effects were the admission of Maine as a free state, the banning of slavery north of the southern border of Missouri (save Missouri itself) in the Louisiana Purchase territory, and the temporary decrease in north-south tensions.

7-L. The Abolitionist Movement

Answers may vary slightly. Abolitionism was the movement to abolish, or end, slavery in the United States. It began in the late 1700s and grew during the 1800s up until the Civil War. Leading abolitionists included William Lloyd Garrison, Frederick Douglass, Charles Hodge, Lucretia Mott, Angelina Grimké, Wendell Phillips, and Sojourner Truth. Most abolitionists lived in the North, particularly New England. Abolitionists spoke, demonstrated, published their views, and lobbied government leaders. The abolition movement is important because it was a major factor in the North-South tensions that led to the Civil War and the eventual abolition of slavery.

7-M. Map Study: The Underground Railroad

Maps will vary depending on the source used, but should accurately reflect the source and include appropriate labels. The caption should demonstrate an understanding of the Underground Railroad as a loose network created to help people escaping slavery.

7-N. The Time Machine: Music

Answers will vary. Generally:

First Half of the 1800s: music was popular, people sang together, people owned instruments, people sang in many settings, slaves would sing spirituals to send messages

Today: all of the 19th-century activities save secret messages in spirituals plus modern developments, especially electronic recording and instruments, new styles of music

Both: all of the 19th-century activities save secret messages in spirituals

7-O. A Postcard from the Past: The John Rankin House National Historic Landmark

Reward research and earnest attempts.

Unit 8

8-A. The Civil War and Reconstruction

Questions will vary, but should be relevant to the unit. Ensure answers are correct.

8-B. The Compromise of 1850

Answers will vary. Major causes of the Compromise of 1850 was the desire to settle the conflict between supporters and opponents of slavery and the acquisition of the Mexican Cession (which had to be declared slave or free). Major results of the Compromise included Texas giving up some territory, the enactment of a strong Fugitive Slave Law, the abolition of slavery in the District of Columbia, the admission of California as a free state, the organization of the Utah and New Mexico territories, and, especially a temporary resolution that delayed the onset of the Civil War.

8-C. Uncle Tom's Cabin

Answers may vary slightly. Cover art should be appropriate.

Effects: inflamed anti-slavery fever

Description: a novel about the suffering of several enslaved people

Year Published: 1852

Written By: Harriet Beecher Stowe

8-D. The Kansas-Nebraska Act

Major causes of the Kansas-Nebraska Act include increased settlement in Midwest and the desire to organize territories in the region. It was a law that organized the territories of Kansas and Nebraska and declared that the people of each territory could decide themselves whether slavery would be allowed in each territory. Major effects of the Act include the overturning of the Missouri Compromise, the increase of tensions between pro- and antislavery forces, the possibility of more slave territory, and, especially, the increased likelihood of a civil war.

8-E. Differences Between North and South

Answers will vary. Generally:

North: free states, urban, educated, liberal, industrial, favoring a strong national government, wealthy, better infrastructure

South: slave states, rural, less educated, conservative, agricultural, favoring states' rights, poorer, weaker infrastructure

Common Facts: culture, language, economic system

8-F. A Nation Divided

Ensure states and territories are labeled correctly.

8-G. Major Events of the Civil War

Entries will vary, but probably should at least include the attack on Fort Sumter, the Battles of Gettysburg and Vicksburg, the Emancipation Proclamation, and the surrender at Appomattox.

8-H. Biography: Abraham Lincoln

Lincoln lived from 1809 to 1865. He was raised in cabins on farms and had little formal schooling. He was honest and hardworking. Descriptive words will vary: tall, brave, smart, etc. His Emancipation Proclamation emancipated, or freed, the slaves. One of his most famous quotations is "government of the people, by the people, for the people." We honor Lincoln through his memorial, a holiday, on the five-dollar bill, and the naming of several towns.

8-I. A Voice from the Past: The Gettysburg Address

Lincoln's main point is that Americans dedicate themselves to winning the war. The country is "conceived in liberty and dedicated to the proposition that all men are created equal." The purpose of the war, Whether a such based on freedom and equality can last.

8-J. Lincoln's Assassination

Captions will vary but should indicate that John Wilkes Booth assassinated Abraham Lincoln.

8-K. Reconstruction

Reconstruction was the period after the Civil War in which rebellious states were readmitted to the union; the union was "reconstructed." The picture shows African-American women and white women working together. Carpetbaggers were white northerners who traveled to the South to help newly freed people. Scalawags were white southerners who had opposed secession and worked to help newly freed people.

8-L. Map Study: The United States in 1870

Maps will vary; check for essential accuracy. Population data: 38.6 million; 74% rural, 26% urban

8-M. The Time Machine: Toys and Games

Answers will vary. Generally:

Middle 1800s: most toys homemade, dolls, hoops, cup-and-ball toys, yo-yos, racing, make believe

Today: all of the 19th-century activities save hoops and toy horses, most toys manufactured, much greater variety, electronic games

Both: all of the 19th-century activities save hoops and toy horses

8-N. A Postcard from the Past: Gettysburg National Military Park

Reward research and earnest attempts.

Assessments

Unit 1 Assessment

A. 1. E 2. B 3. D 4. C 5. A

B. 4, 1, 5, 3, 2

C. Answers will vary but should include the search for a sea route, Columbus's accidental discovery, and then further European exploration and claims.

D. Answers will vary, but should be supported.

Unit 2 Assessment

A. 1. D 2. E 3. A 4. C 5. B

B. 2, 4, 3, 5, 1

C. Answers will vary but should include that the Pilgrims sought religious freedom outside of England and hoped to find it by establishing their own colony in America.

D. Answers will vary, but should be supported.

Unit 3 Assessment

A. 1. D 2. C 3. A 4. E 5. B

B. 3, 5, 2, 1, 4

C. Answers will vary but should include the oppressive actions of the British, especially the Sugar, Stamp, Townshend, and Intolerable Acts.

D. Answers will vary, but should be supported.

Unit 4 Assessment

A. **1.** E **2.** A **3.** B **4.** D **5.** C

B. 5, 4, 1, 3, 2

C. Answers will vary but should refer to the ineffectiveness of the Articles of Confederation due to its failure to create a strong national government.

D. Answers will vary, but should be explained.

Unit 5 Assessment

A. **1.** A **2.** D **3.** E **4.** C **5.** B

B. 1, 4, 2, 3, 5

C. Answers will vary but should include expansion, western trails, settlement, and displacement of Native Americans.

D. Answers will vary, but should be explained.

Unit 6 Assessment

A. **1.** C **2.** A **3.** E **4.** D **5.** B

B. 5, 3, 1, 2, 4

C. Answers will vary but should refer to the economic boom, westward expansion, increased travel, and decreased travel times.

D. Answers will vary, but should be supported.

Unit 7 Assessment

A. **1.** E **2.** C **3.** D **4.** B **5.** A

B. 2, 1, 4, 5, 3

C. Answers will vary but should include their removal to the Indian Territory and their suffering on the Trail of Tears.

D. Answers will vary, but should be explained.

Unit 8 Assessment

A. **1.** C **2.** D **3.** B **4.** E **5.** A

B. 5, 4, 3, 1, 2

C. Answers will vary but should include the division over slavery and states rights and the different cultures of the two regions.

D. Answers will vary, but should be explained.

Made in the USA
Columbia, SC
05 January 2023

75560551R00226